## ALSO BY MARK J. ASHER

# humphrey was here

A dog owner's story of love, loss, and letting go

## BY MARK J. ASHER

**Humphrey Was Here:**
**A dog owner's story of love, loss, and letting go**

ISBN 978-1449580407

Printed and distributed by CreateSpace, a DBA of
On-Demand Publishing, LLC

I write to remember the black rings around his radiant brown eyes and the silklike softness of his coat. The way his right ear neatly folded over, while his left stood at attention. The way he furiously spun in circles of joy when he knew it was "walk time." How he loved sniffing the earth, marking the trees, trying to eat bees, and chasing birds and squirrels. His nighttime routine of jumping on the bed, rolling on his back, pointing his paws toward the ceiling, and demanding love. The way he and I would howl together in a soaring duet at the sound of an approaching fire engine. How he would sit outside the kitchen, with his paws crossed, waiting for his lunchtime bone. How his head would cock and his ears would perk when he heard or saw anything that piqued his curiosity. How his incomparable companionship and unconditional joy saw me through every headache, heartache, triumph, and life transition that I experienced for seven years.

The last time I typed on this laptop, Humphrey was sitting next to me on the couch. Anxious for his dinner and ritual afternoon walk, he began pawing at the laptop keyboard with his big, soft brown paws. He was never one to let you guess his desires or intentions. He used every part of his being—his expressive eyes, powerful body, keen intellect, and good looks—to get anything he wanted. And with a softhearted owner, who was his best friend, big brother, and doting dad, he most often succeeded.

So after a few more moments of writing, followed by a dinner inhaled canine quick, we walked from our tiny studio apartment in the Russian Hill section of San Francisco to a small neighborhood park four blocks away.

Whenever possible, along our route to the park, Humphrey liked to call on his canine-loving clientele, which included store owners and their patrons. Today's target was a stylishly dressed woman in her forties exiting a high-end clothing boutique.

Always conscientious of a stranger's comfort with dogs, I had worked endlessly with Humphrey on not pulling hard on the leash and impulsively darting toward his desires. His desires, expressed daily, were to seek attention from every passerby with two willing hands and, perhaps, a couple of hidden treats. It wasn't that I didn't want Humphrey to meet his quota of pets and bones, I assured him, I was just interested in a safer and softer sell.

Dog trainers insist that behind every well-behaved dog

is a disciplined owner, consistent in implementing the handling instructions they learn while training their dog. I had been diligent with Humphrey during the nine months we had lived in the city, and to my delight he had vastly improved.

Improved, but not quite reformed. After all, Humphrey was a lifelong advocate for rewriting the rules of standard canine behavior. To his way of thinking, they were just a bit too rigid. *Equal rights for canines!* he would protest with a pout that could melt the heart of a dictator. To Humphrey, comprehension of the rules was scholarly, compliance cowardly, if not preceded with a bit of resistance. The life of a happy-go-lucky Lab, dutifully by its owner's side as she pushed her twins in a baby carriage, was not for Humphrey.

As we approached the store, Humphrey was heeling like a show dog in prime form, stopping religiously to mark the trees that served as centerpieces to the small green squares lining the sidewalk. But despite his model behavior, he was actively scanning the area in front of him like a quarterback looking to pick out an open receiver—I could sense that obedience was about to lose out to impulse.

I proved to be right. Just as we passed the front door, Humphrey permanently lengthened my left arm, yanking me in the direction of where the woman was standing. Diplomatically, I pleaded with him to heel: "No, Humphrey, no. You just can't." But in a flash he was at the woman's feet, making his persuasive pitch—*Hi! It's me, Humphrey. Pet me, love me, feed me!*

Luckily the woman was a dog person and the two of them exchanged greetings. She dropped her shopping bags to the ground and knelt beside Humphrey. Like a desperate driver who had just spotted a rare parking place, Humphrey backed his body into hers. As the woman wrapped her arms around him to pet his chest, Humphrey looked back at her with approval and encouragement to continue. When Humphrey finally turned back around to face her, most likely in a plea for treats, the woman asked for Humphrey's paw. Humphrey responded with his paw, his leg, and his shoulder, practically hugging her. She continued to pacify Humphrey while she and I made small talk, rubbing his head and giving him long strokes along his back. Humphrey was beaming up at me, as if to say *See Dad, I told you she wanted to meet me.*

There was also a night version to this routine. With the shops closed, Humphrey focused his efforts on restaurants. Here his contacts were the hostesses that worked at the upscale restaurants lining Polk Street. Many would quickly pop outside to give Humphrey a quick hello and a treat. A sweet gesture, but in Humphrey's mind it was expected, and once you set a routine with Humphrey, he expected full compliance, especially when it related to food.

It could become a bit of a problem if we passed a particular restaurant and his favorite hostess wasn't working. He would stubbornly stand in front of the restaurant demanding a treat from a substitute source or at least an explanation. The patrons with the window seats would get a kick out of watching Humphrey defiantly standing his ground while I tried to convince him to take a rain check and continue walking.

We left Humphrey's new friend at the boutique and continued toward the park. Once there, Humphrey began his usual investigation of sights and smells. In the far corner, after ducking behind a large bush to do his business, he reappeared with a chew toy. Humphrey was very particular about which preowned chew toys he deemed worthy of coveting. In observing his selections, I never understood his criteria. To me they all seemed the same— dirty, decorated with teeth marks, and usually missing a few pieces. But clearly not to an avid chew toy collector like Humphrey. With his expertise and shrewd selection process, he could have written a doggie Blue Book for used chew toys.

The one he had in his grips obviously had great value. You could tell by his antics, reserved for rare finds—a couple of short victory laps with his head held high in the air, juggling the toy in his mouth. After his celebratory strut, he settled down, cradling the toy between his paws, and issued a few introductory licks, before kicking in to full-chew mode. (The dichotomy of a dog toy—cherished one minute, destroyed the next.) Looking around, I was thankful that no other dog in the park had claimed ownership of the toy. That always led to an embarrassing, sticky situation—Humphrey definitely operated with a finders-keepers mentality.

Like a parent at a Little League game, I grabbed a bench and watched my boy. Framed by a soft rectangular patch of sun on the sloping lawn, Humphrey gnawed on, achieving devout oneness with his toy.

A nearby family with two young children and a golden retriever fit for a breeder's brochure got me thinking about Humphrey's role in my life. Seven years before, when my then-wife and I brought him home, he was just a dog, a natural addition to a family portrait in the process of being painted. Now, after a slew of major life changes, he remained the last link to that time, an indispensable companion who had seen me through death, divorce, career change, and relocation.

My nostalgic trance was interrupted by a fascinating game of fetch happening ten yards to my left. The dog owner, a lanky guy in a baseball cap, was slicing a laser beam of red light through the air like an airplane mechanic directing a pilot. The dog, a cute light-brown mutt, was chasing the beam of light as it danced in the grass. You would think the dog would have been frustrated by the graspless game, but he was loving it. I was witnessing the birth of the indestructible, slobberless dog toy.

After twenty minutes darkness began to swallow the small bit of remaining daylight. As families with their young children, and owners with their dogs began to head home, I started leaving the park, calling Humphrey to follow. He remained stoic and steadfast to his toy, not so much as lifting his head in acknowledgment of my voice. This was not unusual behavior for Humphrey—when he fixated on something, he became deaf to discipline.

I walked back to where he was lying and tried to rustle him up to go. But every time I got near, he would spring to his feet, move five feet, plop himself down, and start in again on the chew toy. Finally, after being pleaded with, yelled at, bribed with a bone, and threatened to be left behind, he charged toward me, still clutching his prize.

Clipped on the leash, he pulled me like a gale force wind back to the apartment, ignoring his normal tendency to mark everything in his path. Opening the front door to the apartment building, I let him off the leash and he bolted up the stairs. When the slower, human half of the duo finally made it up the four flights of steep stairs, Humphrey was waiting. I opened the door to our unit, and like a two-year-old with a new toy, he dashed to his bed and continued devouring his toy with ravenous intensity.

An hour later, he was fast asleep on his dog bed, curled up like a cinnamon roll.

Vintage Humphrey—inquisitive, adventurous, smart, and defiant, but always irresistible.

Just two weeks prior, I had called my ex-wife, who had shared Humphrey with me for five years, to tell her he had just turned eight. By canine standards for large breeds, he was entering the senior class; by Humphrey's standards, he was a perpetual puppy with boundless energy, exuberance, and curiosity.

He was shaping up to be like one of those lucky guys you see at your twenty-year high school reunion who looks the same as he did in the senior yearbook. Humphrey had no gray on his muzzle or the slightest sag in his belly.

People found his look intriguing. They would take in his black-ringed brown eyes; his exceptionally soft, short brown coat; his ears, one bowing, the other upright, and wonder what breeds had come together to make him. "What type of dog is he?", "Is he a puppy?", and "What do you feed him to make his coat so soft?" were questions I would hear over and over again in our travels.

By best accounts Humphrey was a German shepherd and chow mix. There were elements of both breeds in his tail, which was speckled with strands of black and arched over his back like a wave about to crash. His tongue was spotted in a ratio of purple to red as land to water on a world map, a possible sign of chow roots. He was shorter than the average German shepherd, slightly taller than a chow. His coat was not a forest of fur, like that of most purebred chows, but was a tad shorter than a German shepherd's.

It seems silly for a dog owner to talk about his dog's intelligence, seeing that one's own dog, by virtue of the bond formed through experience and time, is bound to be their odds-on favorite as the smartest dog they know. That said, I contend that all dogs are not created equal—angels, all of them, but not with the same intelligence level. Some dogs have that something extra, just like people, which sets them apart.

Accepting accusations of bragging about my own dog, I'll proudly say Humphrey was at the top of his pack. He had a responsiveness, an alertness, a presence that was well beyond the average dog. He couldn't talk, but his unmistakable facial expressions clearly translated into thoughts, feelings, and opinions. My convictions were confirmed by the countless instant connections he made with perfect strangers that went beyond "Oh, what a nice dog." Humphrey's good looks drew people in; his indescribable intangibles kept them by his side, showering him with praise and pets.

Humphrey and I were quite similar in personality. I am a typical Virgo—diligent, analytical, and intense; a perfectionist. Humphrey, although born in November, could have been an honorary Virgo. Like me, he was finicky in his likes and dislikes, assertive in his opinions, and stubborn in his views.

When it came to dogs and people, however, Humphrey and I had dramatically different views. Humphrey loved people; I was often reserved, shy, and noncommittal about contacts with strangers, preferring music on my Walkman to idle chatter. I loved dogs; Humphrey, like a typical chow, displayed an air of superiority—*I'll smell you, then I'll decide if I'll allow you to smell me.*

Over time, we pulled each other into our discomfort zones and ultimately stretched our personalities. Through his prodding, or, shall I say, *pulling*, I became more open to people. Once he got past his jealousy of my association with other dogs, Humphrey grew far more playful and appreciative of them.

Ironically, as Humphrey was officially entering his golden years, I was finishing work on a photography book on senior dogs entitled *Old Friends: Great Dogs on the Good Life.* I named Humphrey as my CEO (Canine Executive Officer), and a picture of us together in Golden Gate Park graced the book jacket. Humphrey was certainly deserving of the title, having been my career counselor, sniffing out and pointing me in a new direction professionally.

During the photo shoots for the book, which took place over a two-month period, Humphrey had been an incredible sport, putting up with smelling other dogs on me each day when I came home. That's not to say he didn't give me a hard once-over with his inquisitive eyes when I left clutching my camera bag and an intrusive nose investigation when I returned. But all would be forgotten when he sat next to me on the couch and licked my sore, swollen knees between alternating ice bags.

Photographing fifty-two senior dogs, I got an up-close look at the changes and challenges dogs face as they grow older. I was looking forward to one day seeing my sweet Humphrey join the regal elite of distinguished dogs in their tender years—eyes softened, more measured in their movements, with a touch of gray in their muzzles, but still proud and great companions.

But there was time for that yet. Humphrey and I had a new book to bark about, with plans to barnstorm the country in the fall, plus we were on the growl for a new place with a backyard—or so I thought.

One week later, Humphrey would be gone.

Thanksgiving, along with all the other major holidays, always finds kennels booked well in advance. I had gone back and forth on my Thanksgiving plans and was unsure if I was going to spend it in Southern California, where my fragmented family resides, or in Northern California with close friends. At the last minute I decided on Los Angeles and made a few calls to see if anyone still had openings to board Humphrey.

All the places I had usually boarded him when I left town were booked solid with long waiting lists. A good friend of mine in Los Angeles, Jackie, was housesitting a mansion that a successful Hollywood movie producer had recently purchased but had not yet occupied.

The 1940s house, just below the Getty Center in the Santa Monica Mountains, had previously been the Danish Consulate. It had seven bedrooms, an exquisite backyard with a sloping lawn leading down to a beautiful old stone-deck swimming pool, and a view of Los Angeles I had never glimpsed in all my years of growing up there. Staying there with Jackie felt like being in an old California hotel where you were the only guest.

I was thrilled when Jackie emailed me, saying Humphrey and I could stay with her over Thanksgiving. But a few days later, after mulling over how her cats, Oliver and Boo-Boo, would fare with a dog in the house, she changed her mind, saying, "Mark, I just can't do it. The cats will freak out." She suggested that I look for a place in Los Angeles that could keep him.

After I made a few calls, a place Humphrey had previously stayed in San Francisco gave me the website address for the American Boarding Kennels Association (ABKA), a reputable industry organization that listed member kennels by city and state. On their website, I came upon a place that looked nice in Culver City.

I gave them a call, and using my dry wit questioned Leanne, the soft-spoken lady on the other end of the phone, about the quality of a place that was not yet booked solid for Thanksgiving. She told me a lot of their clientele waits until the last minute and that by the time the holiday rolled around, they'd be full. I peppered her with a few more questions. She responded by telling me that the kennel had been featured on Animal Planet, the all-animals cable TV channel, that the facility was an open kennel with no cages, and that I shouldn't worry—"dogs have fun here."

I filled out their paperwork, booked a reservation, and waited to see if any other opportunities closer to home would come through. During the days leading up to Thanksgiving I asked Jackie several times if she would swing by Culver City to check out the kennel. After much badgering, she confessed that she hadn't made the trip but had spoken to someone at her work that knew of the kennel and the owner.

She put her coworker, Leslie, on the phone and I asked her a couple of questions. Leslie told me most of the dogs she knew that had stayed there had liked it but that for some it offered a little too much stimulation. All in all, she thought it was a place worthy of recommendation. When Leslie put Jackie back on the phone, I poked at her with my sense of humor, a brand that aims for laughter while conveying my feelings and desires.

"Jackie, Thanksgiving is a holiday when we give 'thanks' and this Thanksgiving I give 'thanks' that I have a friend like you, willing to let me and my sweet dog, Humphrey, stay with you."

Well, my humor partially succeeded—she laughed. But it didn't change her mind about having both Humphrey and me stay with her over the holiday.

A few days later, with Humphrey sitting like a king on his dog bed in the cargo cab of my Subaru, we headed for Los Angeles. I decided to take the most direct route from San Francisco to L.A. to make the best time and to try to avoid the afternoon traffic that builds up in Los Angeles faster than ants on a bread crumb. It was no use: Getting through downtown L.A. proved to be murder, and when I finally arrived at the kennel it was dark.

Inside it didn't differ from most of the doggie daycares or overnight facilities I had seen. In the reception room, sparsely decorated with a few wicker chairs and dog trinkets, I was met by two female staff members who were expecting Humphrey. Leanne, with whom I had spoken on the phone, had told me that even though I was coming a long way, it was the kennel's policy to do a personality temperament test on each dog that stayed there. No problem, Humphrey had been through these before at various places and had always easily passed.

The women took us into a large rectangular room and introduced Humphrey to a couple of dogs. Humphrey anxiously ran from one side of the room to the other, continually jumping up on the gate we had just entered through. He made little to no attempt to become acquainted with the other dogs, something that didn't overly concern me because Humphrey had always been coy and cautious when first meeting other dogs.

While his general discomfort in being there made me nervous, I reminded myself he had reacted this way every time I dropped him off at the groomer even though I had been taking him to the same one for over two years. I asked the women if this was normal behavior for new arrivals and one of them said, "Yes, some dogs do act this way until they become acclimated."

But as I stood in the kennel's administrative office after saying good-bye to Humphrey and going over feeding details and contact information, an uneasy feeling came over me. I didn't know if I was just tired and irritable after the long drive from San Francisco or if it was the place itself, but something had me standing there wondering if I should just take him with me and get a room at a Motel 6, which allows dogs.

Even in the best of boarding situations, I was never comfortable leaving Humphrey anywhere. Trusting others, unfortunately, had never come easily to me. Sensing my apprehension, the women tried to reassure me, again, that everything would be okay, and that if I wanted I could come during the day to check on him, even take him out for a while. After a couple more minutes of aired neuroses, I finally relented and left. I got back on the still-crowded freeway and made my way like an ant over the bread crumb.

I spent Thanksgiving with my father and enjoyed the days both before and after the holiday with old friends. I had a particularly interesting day when I went with my child-hood friend, Jeff, whom I've known since I was six, back to our old neighborhood. We knocked on the doors of the homes we each had grown up in and hadn't been back to in twenty-eight years.

The people who lived in "my house" were the same couple who had bought it from my parents after their divorce. They had come from Chicago, which ironically was where my family had moved from to build the house. They were accommodating, easygoing people and let Jeff and I wander through the house. They graciously listened to our countless silly stories of innocence and youth.

Next door, at "Jeff's house," we were met with quite a different response. When we approached the house, the woman who lived there was unpacking groceries from the trunk of her car. As we approached, she guardedly said, "Can I help you?" Jeff and I quickly dove into the whole story of who we were and told her that we had just come from her neighbor's.

After our rapid-fire rambling, one would have thought we were innocent enough, if not a little crazy. Reticently, she led us to the front door and into the house, which was unrecognizable from our childhood. As I approached the bedroom area of the house, she gave me a nonverbal stop sign. We wished we were able to see more, but we were thankful for a glimpse inside.

Every day I called the kennel to check on Humphrey and see how he was adjusting. Each person I spoke to over the first three days said Humphrey was enjoying himself and all was well. I thought about going by and taking him out for the day, but I figured it would only be disruptive to take him out, have him think we were going home, and then bring him back to the kennel. Besides, our stay in Los Angeles was more than halfway over.

Time passed quickly as it always does when you're visiting your hometown and there are so many people to see. It was hard to believe that five days had passed and it was time to pick up Humphrey. On my last morning, I enjoyed an extended bull session over coffee with two lifelong friends, Mike and Rob. Afterward, Rob and I walked back to his house, where I had been gathering my stuff together to leave. As we approached the front door Danielle, Rob's wife, had a cordless phone in her hand and a worried look on her face. She told me to immediately call Jackie. Grabbing the phone, I dialed Jackie's number.

"Is something wrong with Humphrey?" I asked, my stomach churning and hands trembling.

Beginning to cry, she said, "I don't know, just call the kennel, please."

"Is he dead?" I blurted out.

"I think so."

I called the kennel with Rob and Danielle standing by my side. Leanne answered the phone, registered that it was me, and began to slowly speak.

"Mark, one of the workers found Humphrey this morning."

"What happened?"

"We don't know. Apparently he threw up last night at 11 P.M., but seemed fine afterward."

I don't remember the rest of the conversation or if there was much more of one. The next thing I knew I was in the passenger seat of Rob's car, heading south on the freeway to see Humphrey. When we pulled up to the kennel, I rushed inside. One of the employees led me to Leanne, who ushered me into a room where Humphrey was covered with a blanket. I told her I needed time alone with him and she left the room.

I slowly rolled back the blanket to see his face. He

looked as sweet as ever, as though he was just taking a nap. Nothing seemed outwardly wrong except that his stomach looked unusually distended. I didn't know what to say to him. I wasn't prepared for a good-bye speech. I was numb. I don't remember if I rolled the blanket back over his face or not.

In an instant I was out on the street walking as fast as I could in any direction. My vision was narrow and cloudy, my insides were a jumbled fog of disbelief, rage, and questions.

When I finally came back to the kennel, Leanne was talking with Jackie, who had just arrived, and Rob. Leanne asked me if I had a vet where I wanted Humphrey taken. I mumbled something to the effect of "no." Jackie, Rob, and Leanne continued talking, occasionally asking me a question. I couldn't digest the reality of the words I was hearing—*autopsy, transport, body.*

After they worked out the details—Leanne agreed that the kennel would pay for all fees incurred as a result of Humphrey's death—Leanne offered to take Humphrey to be examined by a vet who treated her own pets. I agreed and went home with Jackie where I spent the next several hours in her living room pacing and rambling.

*What the hell happened?*

*How could he just die so suddenly?*

*Did the kennel have anything to do with it?*

*This never would have happened if I were with him!*

*Why didn't I listen to my intuition and take him to a motel?*

This was not Humphrey's time to die!

Every half hour I called the emergency animal hospital to see if they had examined Humphrey. Every time the same woman answered, she put me on hold for a couple of minutes, and returned with the same story: "The doctor will call you when he knows something."

Apologizing profusely, Jackie said she absolutely had to leave for a couple hours to take care of something important.

Twenty minutes later, as I paced back and forth outside the front of the house, the cordless phone rang. It was Dr. Travers from the hospital.

"I'm sorry about your dog," he said calmly, with a voice accustomed to delivering bad news. "But at least we know what happened."

*At least we know what happened,* I repeated cynically back to myself. *My dog is dead!*

"Humphrey died of stomach torsion or what some people refer to as bloat or stomach twist," Dr. Travers informed me.

"But how... how can that be? How does this happen?"

"Gastric torsion occurs when a dog has too much exertion after eating. If they ingest too much air from excessive barking, drink too much water or get too much exercise soon after eating, the stomach can turn on its axis and suffocate them."

"Was the kennel at fault?" I asked as I took in the horror of what had happened to my poor Humphrey. "Was there a lot of food in his stomach?"

"A fair amount, but not that much," Dr. Travers responded.

"Is this a common thing, Dr. Travers?"

"Yes, I see quite a bit of it here. Certain breeds—poodles, German shepherds—are more susceptible to it."

When I hung up the phone I went on the attack—on myself. For every prosecuting voice that sprung into my head, I tried to find a defense.

*It was a bad place—I never should have left him at a place he had never been before.*

But when Rob and Jackie walked through earlier today, they said all the dogs were having a great time.

*Jackie's friend Leslie, who knew of the place, told you that it provided a little too much stimulation for some dogs.*

But how could I have known that "too much" meant Humphrey would die?

*When you left him there, you should have sensed he didn't want to be there.*

But Humphrey would shake like a leaf and bolt for the door every time I left him anywhere.

*How could you, the most overprotective dog owner, not have known about this potentially fatal affliction?*

Even if I had known it existed, what are the chances

that Humphrey would actually die from it?

A few hours later Faye, the owner of the kennel, left a voicemail on Jackie's answering machine. She was crying. "We all feel so terrible here—I wish it were one of my own dogs," she said.

When I mustered the strength, later that evening, I called Faye at home. She told me that she had been to the kennel over the Thanksgiving holiday and had met and played with Humphrey. She reassured me that he was having a great time and that he had met a couple of new four-legged friends. She reiterated what Leanne had said—that he had thrown up at around 11 P.M. but seemed fine afterward.

From the second I learned of this disaster—when I wasn't wracked with guilt—I had been suspicious of the kennel's role in Humphrey's death. I tried to counter my suspicions by telling myself it wouldn't have made any sense for Faye and Leanne to freely volunteer the information about Humphrey's problematic last night—especially in these litigious times—if there had been any foul play.

Faye went on to tell me that she had helped many friends—including one whose dog had recently been hit by a car—get through this incredibly difficult time. She joked that with all the friends she's helped, she should become a grief counselor to people who have lost pets.

I told her I wanted to come by her home and talk. She

graciously agreed and told me she would do anything to help. What I didn't tell Faye is that I wanted to know that where Humphrey had spent his last days was a place deeply committed to loving and caring for dogs. And that I had done the best I could for him. I knew she couldn't change the outcome of what had happened, but something inside me told me to go see her.

That night I had a dream about Humphrey.

He furiously wrestles me for the tennis ball, which I'm holding by an attached nylon string. After I pry it loose from his tenacious grip, he waits with darting eyes and adrenaline-filled legs for me to toss the ball down the long hallway. Off he goes—scurrying so fast on the wood floor that he momentarily runs in place before taking off—but he never returns the ball. He proudly clutches it in his mouth, nylon string dangling, as I chase him around the coffee table. After a bit of playful banter, I finally corner him on his bed, where he lies on his back, ball in mouth, happily receiving his reward for being the silliest, most devilish dog in the whole world—belly rubs.

Faye lived near the kennel, and passing the building on the way to her house made my stomach sink. The neighborhood seemed to be in transition from not-so-nice to up-and-coming. Faye's house appeared neat and well maintained.

Her two yellow Labs greeted me as I walked through the open door. It was nice to be in the company of dogs after not being among any during my stay in Los Angeles. I got down on my knees and simultaneously rubbed both of their heads while they lunged to lick my face. As I looked up, Faye was walking toward us. She welcomed me with a smile and a hug. She was in her mid-to-late forties, with blond hair and skin that had seen too much sun. My instinct told me that in her younger days she was the life of the party—bubbly, fun, and flirtatious—but that those days were past her.

As we walked through the living room, I was transfixed by the incredible collection of dog-themed items that littered her home—there were dog pillows, dog dolls, dog books, dog blankets, and countless other dog tchotchkes. I entered the den and sat down on her couch, sandwiched between her two Labs. As her adopted two-year-old daughter split her time between watching *A Bug's Life* and me, we began to talk.

I asked her questions about her life and her business. "How long have you owned the kennel?"

"It's been five years now," she replied. "People who love dogs are always envious of what I do. They mistakenly think that it's easy. It's been a rewarding business, but let me tell you, it ain't easy."

"Has anything like what happened to Humphrey ever happened there before?"

"There was one dog that stayed with us years ago—the owner picked him up, fed him at home, took him for a short walk, and shortly after he got stomach bloat and died."

I was shocked to hear this type of story, and surprised that she would share it with me. Clearly, she was open and honest.

"Do you still spend a lot of time there?" I asked.

"Not as much as in the beginning. I'm into breeding now."

We broke from the conversation and walked out to her backyard patio, which was enclosed by a canvas tent. There, squirming in their playpen, were a bundle of newly born, fuzzy yellow Lab pups. They were all adorable, but Faye instructed me they were not yet ready to be touched. Looking over the litter, I wondered to myself which ones would develop into unique and extraordinary dogs, like Humphrey had. More importantly, I wished them all good homes with loving owners.

When we walked back inside I talked about Humphrey. As Faye looked at some pictures I had recently taken of him, I explained how much closer our bond had become in the years since my wife and I had split. I told her I had thought he was indestructible and launched into the infamous story of how Humphrey had fallen out of a moving car.

The incident occurred when Humphrey was maybe a year and a half old. He relished every chance he got to ride the wind—ears flapping, tongue dangling—as he hung out the back window of my Maxima. We had an ongoing battle as to how far down I would roll the window. Naturally, Humphrey, the young daredevil, wanted nothing but blasting wind on his face. I, the neurotic parent, preferred a more cautious arrangement.

One hot summer afternoon while we were driving up a steep, winding grade, to my horror, I turned to see that Humphrey had fallen out of the window on the last turn. I immediately swerved to the side of the road, flew out of my car, and found him shaken, but incredibly, suffering only a scraped right front paw. I sat with him on the side of the road, checking to see if applying pressure on his legs caused him any pain. He seemed completely fine, but to be sure, I took him to the vet. Thankfully, everything checked out okay.

I felt incredibly fortunate that there were no cars directly behind me at the moment Humphrey took the spill. From then on, much to his dismay, I insisted on vehicles with enclosed back cabs.

Faye was doing her best to try to ease the incredible guilt I was feeling about Humphrey's loss. She told me I had done my best and that Humphrey was lucky to have an owner that cared so deeply. I thanked her but knew the road to forgiveness, when the one I had to forgive was myself, was going to be a long and painful one. After all, Humphrey was not autonomous: I was his protector, his parent, and my lapse of judgment had led to his death.

I thanked Faye for allowing me to visit and said my good-byes to the two Labs and her daughter.

As I drove away, the pit in my stomach was still there, but I felt good about my decision to meet Faye. She seemed to be honest about what had happened to Humphrey, and surely her heart, where dogs were concerned, was in the right place.

A few days later I received a piece of mail that would seriously challenge my feelings. The envelope was sent to me at Jackie's address, and when I opened the card that was enclosed, my first thought was, *How nice, Faye sent me a condolence card.* But as I unfolded the piece of paper lying inside the card, I was horrified. It was a bill from the vet where Humphrey's autopsy had been performed. I was enraged.

First they tell me that they'll pay for everything, then they send me a bill...inside a damn condolence card! This proves that this is a shoddy operation. God damn, why did I leave Humphrey there?

I was too heated to call Faye right away to address the issue. When I called the next morning, she coyly defended her action, saying, "Well...I just wanted you to have a record of what happened to him, where he was at." Whatever her intentions were, her explanation wasn't comforting, nor believable.

While I was at her house she had mentioned that the staff at the kennel was surprised I was not more irate with them after Humphrey's death. Faye must have thought she could send me the bill in a casual way and that I would dutifully pay it.

A month later the $100 deposit I had put down to hold Humphrey's reservation was still on my credit card. I called Leanne, who had taken the reservation, and she promised to make the necessary correction.

In the wake of this awful tragedy, pettiness over money poured salt on my raw wound.

I had endured the surreal and painful odyssey of death before. Five years earlier I had experienced the death of my business partner, Steve, who was just thirty-five years old. He had seemed perfectly normal that day, no different from any other time during our eight years of co-owning a courier service that catered to the entertainment industry. On my way home from work that evening, I received a call from Ken, a buddy of Steve's who had gathered with him and a group of friends to watch Monday night football. Ken told me Steve had suffered a massive heart attack. He was lying dead at UCLA Medical Center.

A week earlier my grandfather had passed away at ninety-four. The only other death I had experienced was when my grandmother (his wife) passed when I was twelve years old. I remember sitting in my room after I got the news from my parents. I knew I was supposed to feel sad, but since my grandma had lived her whole life in Chicago and we had never spent much time together, I didn't feel much.

Steve's death was unexpected and horrific—I was overwhelmed with grief. At Steve's funeral I had to be held upright by my wife while I sobbingly spoke of what a selfless friend and ethical businessman he had been. I cried every morning while getting ready for work and sorely missed his presence every day at the office.

With Steve gone, his family and I decided to sell the business. After six months of dealing with accountants, attorneys, business brokers, and thick emotions, the business was sold.

I never could have imagined that I would encounter another premature death of a close friend only a few years later.

In the spring of 2000, Larkin, a friend and coworker, choked to death at twenty-nine. On the Saturday she died we had plans to go to a street festival on Fillmore Street in San Francisco, and I became concerned when she didn't return my multiple phone calls. I was stunned when I walked into work on Monday morning and was met with several coworkers flooding out of the office in tears after learning of Larkin's death.

When I had joined the company, Larkin was the first one to walk over to my cubicle and welcome me, the first one to invite me to lunch with her close group of coworkers, the first one to take an interest in how my transition was going. We had a common thread in that she had grown up in Ventura, California, a short distance from Ojai, where I had previously lived.

Our company sent Jessica, another coworker, and me to attend Larkin's funeral in a beautiful Mission-style church in Santa Barbara. One after another Larkin's friends stood at the pulpit, pouring out memories. Each story touched on Larkin's joyful spirit, uncommon generosity, eclectic taste, and creativity.

With more people paying their respects to Larkin than the church could accommodate, I was unable to approach her parents to offer my condolences. Instead I wrote a letter, which I sent to them shortly after the funeral, explaining how much their daughter's friendship had meant to me.

Months later, her parents came up from Southern California to see where Larkin had worked. They sought me out and thanked me for writing the letter. Larkin had shared many stories with me about how rare her bond was with her family. The grief of losing a child is immeasurable and lifelong, but when the parents are genuinely close to a child when she becomes an adult, the grief must be that much greater. It was reflected in the faces of her parents, who were the most broken people I had ever seen.

I'd like to say that both of these traumatic experiences,

with unexpected loss at a young age, prepared me for Humphrey's death, but they did not. There is no advanced degree in dealing with death—only a long, painful passage from pitch-black darkness to eventual flickers of light. What follows is my journey.

Waking up at Jackie's in the days that followed Humphrey's death I was besieged by shock and anger.

I simply couldn't believe that he was gone. That I would never be able to take walks with him again through the wooded and wonderful trails of the Presidio, or wrestle with him on the living room floor, or give him his beloved belly pets before bedtime, or wake again to his brown eyes, enthusiastically pulling me into a new day.

I was boiling with anger, both at myself and, increasingly, at the world, for taking away the thing I loved the most.

If it was God's will, I wanted to know how he dispersed his tragedies—an immediate investigation of his (or her) distribution system was in order. If I had bad karma, I demanded to know what I had done in another life. I traced back through my entire life, trying to identify some behavior, some action, some incident, that could have precipitated Humphrey's fate. If everything happened for a reason, I wanted to know the reason now, when the pain was intense.

I wanted answers; I kept coming up with more questions.

For the first time in my life, I couldn't be alone. I felt myself transformed from a lifelong homebody into someone who needed to be in constant motion. I ran from reality at warp speed; calm and quiet, my normal, steady companions, became dreaded visitors. Running on the adrenaline of avoidance and the fumes of anger, I stumbled, showerless, unshaven, and tired, from one moment to the next, from one place to another.

While friends went on with their lives, I spent my mornings at bookstores, poring over books on spirituality, religion, depression, death, and anything else that could help me make sense of the senseless.

I found solace in stories that illustrated people's courage in coping with tragic, unforeseen circumstances. But nowhere did I find the answer to the question that was burning inside me: Why do the good die young? After experiencing the deaths of three of the sweetest souls I had known—Steve, Larkin, and Humphrey—I could only surmise that there must be a better place than here on Earth, and that the most selfless and compassionate among us get to go there first.

I pictured a place where dogs ran in endless green fields with giant bone dispensers in every direction. When the dogs got tired of running, there were countless human hands to pet them to their hearts' content.

Dogs were everywhere—hotels, restaurants, stores—and there was nowhere they weren't welcome. Behind the wheel of the car next to you, a standard poodle; the bank manager, a distinguished golden retriever; the tireless field reporter bringing you the breaking news, an energetic German shepherd/chow mix named Humphrey.

In the afternoons, I went by my old elementary school and struck up a conversation with the principal as she was leaving for the day; I visited my old high school and reminisced about my final and best year there; I sat in the home team's dugout where I once played Little League and stared out onto the field. Anything to take my mind away.

For a few moments I was able to suspend the sad reality of what had happened to Humphrey. After all, I was still away from home, in a place I didn't associate with him. Humphrey wasn't supposed to be with me. I was still on vacation, I thought to myself. Soon I'd be going to pick him up. Somewhere Humphrey anxiously awaited me.

In the early evening, I would have dinner with a friend and then see a movie or head back to the bookstore, where I'd stay until closing. Other times, I stopped by my father's and sat in his smoke-filled living room, watching TV and talking. If all my options ran dry, I would drive aimlessly, in intense traffic, out of the Valley, into the city, and back again, hoping to forestall the sad, awful feeling I would face when I stopped.

But it was never long before the stimulus of day would give way to the silence of night. And there the awfulness of Humphrey's last hours would crowd my mind and crush my heart. As I lay in bed, thoughts of him, suffering for hours without a chance for help, haunted me. The thoughts were too painful to keep out and too painful to let in. A continuous loop of unanswerable questions would cycle through my mind: *Why did I have to lose Humphrey? Why on Earth didn't I listen to my own voice and take him away from the kennel? Why?*

When I couldn't sleep, I would get out of bed and search the Internet for more information on the ailment that had befallen my dog. But as much as I wanted to learn more, there was a part of me that didn't want to know, that just couldn't face the gruesome details, that wanted to remember Humphrey as he lived, not as he died.

Before long a new tactic in dealing with Humphrey's death crept into my consciousness—I began to rationalize Humphrey's importance to me. I began telling myself, or I should say *selling* myself, that if I had a richer, fuller life, if I were still married and still had a house, that Humphrey's death wouldn't be as painful. The problem, I decided, was that my life was out of balance. I had become too attached to my dog, had begun to count too much on his role in my life.

Friends echoed these sentiments, saying that perhaps Humphrey's death was a signal to me to "get on with my life." That maybe it was high time for me to move past my divorce, find someone new, and start a new life.

I anticipated the inevitable "It's only a dog" comments and waited at the ready with an artillery of words:

*Look, Humphrey was with me every day, almost every hour. We woke together, walked together, worked together, explored together, played together, and slept together. I've experienced loss before, but not like this. Humphrey was part of my internal space. I'm sick and tired of people trying to minimize the death of a dog or an animal in comparison to the death of a human. Death is death. It's loss, grief. And besides, humans can't give us what dogs do, and vice versa.*

I'm happy to say I never had to use these words.

Rationalizations don't change reality, I soon reminded myself. And the reality is that for who I was, given the place I was in my life, Humphrey was my brightest light, bringing forward the best part of me. From then on, thankfully, I never again diminished his role in my life or denied myself the honest pain that came from his death.

As days went by it became increasingly difficult for me to stay at Jackie's. When she would leave for work in the morning I was left alone in a huge, silent house. It didn't take long for me to look out on the sprawling lawns in the front and back and imagine Humphrey, alive and well, frolicking about.

I didn't blame Jackie—she had had her reasons for not allowing Humphrey and me to stay with her—but it was impossible not to think that if she had let us stay, then Humphrey...

The what-if scenarios became unbearable.

Dr. Elisabeth Kübler-Ross, the original guru of grief, defined the process of grieving as a five-stage process involving denial, anger, bargaining, depression, and acceptance. One passes through the stages in no particular order and can find oneself at any stage, at any time, while dealing with death.

In the bargaining stage a grieving person attempts to negotiate the outcome of a death by ruminating on things they might have done to prevent it. Kübler-Ross refers to this stage as a "temporary truce." But with five places or people that could have cared for Humphrey, instead of *that* kennel over that dreadful Thanksgiving holiday, popping into my head every couple of hours—scenarios that would have kept him alive—the bargaining phase for me had become a "temporary living hell."

I tortured friends around me with endless conversations of what could have been, if only. They responded with saintlike listening skills, reassurances I had done my best, temporary remedies, suggestions ("get a new dog"), and social plans. But nothing could interrupt the war I was waging against myself for allowing Humphrey to die outside of my watch, my control, my care.

I felt I needed to leave Jackie's, but where would I go?

I contemplated going back to San Francisco, but even

with Humphrey alive, my first crack at city living had been a cold and lonely experience. I had moved there for logical reasons—a lower rent than what I had been paying and closer proximity to business contacts and friends. But I sorely missed the towering trees and sweet smells of nature Humphrey and I enjoyed in Mill Valley, a rustic town just across the Golden Gate Bridge where we had previously lived. The only plus to our experience in the city—a nearby park with a patch of green and plenty of pooches for Humphrey to play with—was offset by the path of broken glass, debris, and exhaust-belching buses you had to navigate in order to get there.

With Humphrey now gone, my apartment would be an unbearably empty place filled with painful reminders of his absence. Besides, I now only had a little over a month left on my lease, and the longer I stayed away, the more I felt I would most likely go back only to pack up my belongings.

Since Humphrey's death, Rob had graciously offered me a spot on his couch for as long as I needed it. Certainly it would have been my first choice. Rob and I had remained close friends since we were six years old, when his family moved from the East Coast, and mine from the Midwest, to the same suburb in Southern California. He knew the long troubled history of my family and had helped steer me through every harrowing turn of my life. He understood, as well as anyone, how much Humphrey had meant to me.

But Rob's place was busting at the seams with two young children, a stay-at-home mom who ran a business out of the garage, and Rob, a writer who worked from home. Needless to say, they didn't need the added burden of a grown man who was hopelessly sad, deeply depressed, and crying a lot.

I called him up and broached the subject again—pressing hard against his always inviting personality to make sure he and his wife were still okay with the idea. He insisted it was no problem and assured me (even though I didn't believe him) that he would let me know when I had worn out my welcome.

One day soon after I arrived, Rob's seven-year-old daughter, Olivia, handed me a stuffed-animal dog with a note attached to its collar. Rob was touched by his daughter's empathy toward me and encouraged me to open the note. But just seeing the stuffed animal put me on the verge of breaking down. I couldn't bear to read the note.

Days later, my friend Jeff stopped by with his wife, Kim, and their kids. Having heard from his parents what had happened, Griffin, their three-year-old, came up to me and asked, "What happened to your dog? Why don't you live with your dog anymore?" I was speechless—Kim had to pick up the conversation for me.

It killed me to be so sad in front of my friends'

children. I wished I could put on a happier face, but even my best acting skills (which aren't very good) couldn't hide my grief.

The days continued to go by in a blur, a painful haze of disbelief, anger, and depression.

It's in these moments when you are at your most vulnerable, that things happen that leave you wondering whether you've lost your mind or if you're simply in the right place to receive them.

Two such incidents, similar in nature, happened to me over a two-day period.

The first occurred while I was driving down Ventura Boulevard, a crowded artery that runs through the San Fernando Valley and is littered with cars, pedestrians, and shops. I was in the passenger seat of Rob's car, running an errand, when I looked over to the lane just left of us and saw a soulful pit bull mix riding shotgun in the passenger seat of an old white van. The dog must have been standing on an armrest between the passenger and driver seats because it was propped pretty high up. The dog locked eyes with me and would not let go.

Now, I love dogs and have had plenty of contact with them in the years since acquiring Humphrey—but this was different. This dog's gaze was so powerful it was as if it was looking inside me. Was the dog trying to send me some type of message from Humphrey, I wondered? Ridiculous, I reasoned with myself, turning away as we continued down the boulevard. It's nothing more than my vivid imagination playing tricks on me.

Minutes later I turned back, and there was the pit bull, still alongside us in the white van, meeting my gaze! It wasn't as though the dog would momentarily take its eyes off me and glimpse at the oncoming road or glance for a second at its owner—its eyes were locked on me in an unmistakable way. This lasted for another four blocks or so before we made a right turn and lost sight of the van.

The following day I was standing with Jackie at an intersection, waiting for the light to change, when I saw a German shepherd in the back seat of a white convertible. The car was stopped in traffic and was smack in the middle of the crosswalk. The dog was staring intently at me. I didn't say anything, just smiled back. But ten seconds later, Jackie said, "Mark, isn't it weird the way that dog keeps staring at you?" Well, at least I knew this time it wasn't my imagination.

The German shepherd continued to look at me, unfazed by my short exchange with Jackie. Then, just as the car began to pull away, the dog let out two quick barks.

I don't pretend to know what either incident meant, but I'd like to think that since Humphrey and I didn't have a chance for a formal farewell, he was finding a way to send me a final message of love.

As the holiday season arrived, another accommodation

option arose. Jeff was leaving with his family for a one-week trip to Mexico. I graciously accepted his offer for seven days of solitude in their empty house. It would be the perfect impetus I needed to get back into my routine, sort out my thoughts, and figure out what was next.

The first night alone in the normally rambunctious living quarters of a three-year-old boy and a six-year-old girl felt strange. It was as if I had just rented a large vacation home and was awaiting my family to spend the holidays. Toys were neatly collected in the corner of the living room. The kitchen was well stocked and clean. The long shelf above the fireplace, as well as the nearby entertainment center, were blanketed with holiday cards.

The world outside my door, the next morning, however, was a familiar one. The gated community Jeff lived in was not unlike the one we had grown up in (minus the gate). It was predominantly made up of young, white, and affluent families, most with newborns and young children. The major difference between then and now was the presence of bigger, brighter, and louder toys; architecturally identical monster homes; tanklike automotive vehicles; and twelve-year-old girls that looked like miniatures of their provocatively dressed, stylish moms. Modern suburbia had been on consumption steroids for thirty years and it showed.

Not surprisingly, on my daily walks, I bumped into a host of familiar faces—an old next-door neighbor, an ex-girlfriend I hadn't seen in ten years, a baseball buddy who was on my Little League team for several years. I chatted with each for a while, reminiscing about old times.

When the conversation turned to the present day, family life was the dominant topic. After learning the names and ages of their children, and viewing pictures they had of them in their wallets and purses, I was evasive about my own life. I didn't feel compelled to share the news about Humphrey, seeing that none of them had mentioned that they had a dog. I figured it would be impossible for a person with a family but no dog to understand the connection Humphrey and I shared and the void his death had created in my life.

There was, however, no shortage of dogs in the neighborhood, and seeing them was extremely difficult on me. There was just something about seeing someone walk their dog that tore me apart. It was a painful reminder of a bond that I had lost and missed dearly.

I wanted to walk up to every dog owner I saw and tell them Humphrey's story. I wanted to make sure they loved their dog like there was no tomorrow, because sometimes there isn't one. I wanted them to know that soon enough—too soon—a dog's life passes. If they had children, I wanted to ensure they weren't neglecting their dog while fulfilling their parental responsibilities. Instead, I remained silent, staring from across the way, wishing it were my dog out on a morning walk, looking back at me with giddy joy.

The week went by lazily and was uneventful. My constant running had slowed down, as I spent most of my time at the house reading, writing, and watching TV. My mind, however, was still spinning at a furious pace, trying to grasp what had happened to Humphrey and why.

The mind is a tricky thing. It can lead you to believe that if you sound something out enough, you can make it okay. But the heart is unmoved by endless analysis. Nothing can dissipate without time and tears.

While watching TV in the living room on one of my last afternoons before my stay was over, I heard a commotion coming from the next-door neighbor's yard. Peeking through the kitchen blinds, I glimpsed one of life's most joyous moments—the arrival of a new puppy. The dog, a black Lab, looked like a large cat from where I stood. As it bounced around its new environment, the family—two parents pushing forty and their two young daughters—gushed on.

Through the closed window, I could hear them playing the name game. "How about 'Josie'?" the father said. "No, that's corny. I like the name 'Ella,'" the mother piped in. "I want her to be 'Abby,'" the youngest daughter interjected. The discussion continued. I walked back into the living room, put my feet up on the couch, and thought back to Humphrey's first days.

Names are strange. Most times we name pets and people before we know their personalities. And many times their personalities end up reflecting their names.

"Humphrey" is a perfect example. My ex-wife, Lori, named him the day we brought him home—long before we knew he would hump every dog he encountered during the first two years of his life. There was nothing in particular that directed Lori to the name, our new puppy just seemed like a good Humphrey.

At the time we got Humphrey, Lori and I had been dating for six months, with plans to eventually marry, and in two weeks we would be moving from our apartment in Santa Monica to our first home. A dog seemed like a natural next step.

Not that I was new to dogs. I had grown up with a poodle named Pumpkin. She was small with a poufy mound of fur on her head and a short bushy tail. Pumpkin's defining characteristic was her lush beard, most often darker in color from the rest of her caramel-colored coat as a result of being dipped into water and food bowls. I remember thinking as a kid it was silly that a girl dog had a beard.

My sweetest memory of Pumpkin is coming home from school every day and finding her bathed in a stream of sunlight on my bedroom floor. (Her theme song must have been the Beatles' "I'll Follow the Sun"—wherever the sun was, you could find Pumpkin.) I don't recall taking her for many walks or ever throwing her a ball. For a young dog, she wasn't particularly spunky or playful. She never, to my recollection, sought attention from anyone in particular. Pumpkin just existed. Perhaps like myself she was just trying to survive my family environment.

That environment consisted of two adults who had great disdain for one another and a son and daughter, two years apart, who rarely spoke. And amidst the anger of a broken marriage that had yet to break apart, poor Pumpkin sometimes paid the price. For no apparent reason that I can remember, my father hated Pumpkin. Every time she came across his path, he would swat her with a newspaper or chase her down the hallway. He yelled at Pumpkin as much as he yelled at my mother.

When I was twelve, my parents divorced. (At the time I cried like a baby, but if I could have clearly seen how poorly suited they were for one another, I would have thrown a party.) Not long after, I came home from school one day to find that my mother had given Pumpkin away. Easily and often overwhelmed, my mother wasn't one to explain things. She never told me where Pumpkin had gone and why she had decided to get rid of her. I vaguely remember being confused and a little upset.

I wish I could have one day to spend with Pumpkin to learn more about her and give her the love she deserved and never got. I realize now how much Pumpkin could have helped comfort me in the unhappy, turbulent times that defined my childhood, but for whatever reason we never bonded in a way that led me to be a dog lover.

A six-month-old German shepherd/chow mix was ready and willing to take me to the next level of appreciation for man's best friend.

For the longest time when people asked me where we got Humphrey, I told them, "We adopted him...from a shelter in Santa Monica." The truth, that he came from a pet store in Santa Monica, embarrassed me after I came to learn about puppy mills and the plight of countless dogs sitting in animal shelters in need of good homes.

In time I came to realize it didn't matter where he came from, it mattered what he came with. And although that would ultimately become more than I could ever imagine, it didn't seem like much when Lori and I let this six-month-old puppy, whom the pet store called Bear, loose in our one-bedroom apartment.

Let's just say he didn't make a subtle entrance. For two solid weeks, he was a blur of fur, a maniac in motion. You just couldn't stop him long enough to look into his eyes and search his soul for any measure of kindness. He didn't take well to any interaction, and correcting his behavior was futile. Lori and I were actually scared of him at first.

Lori's mother, Noel, who was visiting from Massachusetts at the time, watched with bemusement, suggesting we assert our alpha dog superiority. Alpha dog, smalpha dog—Humphrey was in a pack of his own. And while part of his behavior could be chalked up to being a puppy, I was convinced he had a screw loose. I nicknamed him the Brown Bomber.

Whenever we left Humphrey for brief periods, he would destroy, at a revenger's pace, the plastic baseboard around the perimeter of the bathroom, where we would leave him with newspaper to catch any urges he might have. The pet store recommended that we spray a product called Bitter Apple on the areas he was chewing. Humphrey was unimpressed by the powerful language on the label. The product didn't slow his progress—or destruction, as it were—one bite.

Luckily, before Humphrey ate any further into our security deposit, we moved into our new home in Ojai, a small community an hour north of Los Angeles.

The funky pink cinderblock house, built in 1953, was long on charm but short on practicality. Every repairman that worked on our home, and there were many over the years, was befuddled by its shoddy construction—"In all my years of doing this, I've never seen one built like that before!"

But the house sat on an acre of land, and the backyard, with its park-size swatch of unmanicured open space, a swimming pool, eight giant oak trees, and a fruit stand's worth of fruit trees, quickly became Humphrey's domain. It was the perfect outlet for his constant energy and his insatiable desire to explore every inch of his environment.

He would begin each day by surveying the perimeter of the property, like a shopkeeper taking inventory, marking and inspecting his terrain. By afternoon he would be running long looping circles, using the furthest oak tree and the pool as his anchor points, in the pursuit of nothing but wind and exhilaration. Our friends would marvel at his raw energy, speed, and athletic agility as he gracefully navigated everything in his path. By dusk, after the excitement of the day had died down, he would lie on an old rickety bench beneath the apricot tree and stare meditatively at the mountains in the distance.

Humphrey was in heaven—he had land to roam, dirt to dig, and a pair of humans who treated him like a royal son.

He soon discovered the first great nemesis of his life—squirrels. They were abundant in our backyard and would prove to be a daunting foe for Humphrey, providing him with endless challenges.

This canine version of a cat-and-mouse game would start simply enough, with Humphrey resting peacefully on the swimming pool deck. But once he would hear the squirrels chirping away beneath the oak trees, the sleeping giant would awaken. He would slowly get up, creep a few feet to the edge of the deck, pause to plot his attack route, and then BAM!—a split second later, Humphrey would be at the base of the oak tree, looking up at the squirrels, who would be gleefully taunting him from the large limbs above.

Humphrey would instantly launch into an aural assault that included a mix of barking and whimpering, before circling the tree to reassess the position of his prey. He would then patiently wait, motionless, sometimes for as long as ten minutes, for the squirrels to make their next move.

When a brave squirrel would finally make a mad dash from the oak tree, Humphrey would be in hot pursuit, inches from the terrorized creature's tail. But once the cloud of dust cleared, the squirrel would be victoriously chirping from atop a telephone line, far from Humphrey's reach.

Distraught but never defeated, Humphrey repeated the same tiring exercise every couple of days. He never did catch a squirrel, to my knowledge, and even went so far as to scale an apricot tree in pursuit of his bushy-tailed prey.

Humphrey's fierce bravado was only a small part of his personality—he was far more grace and sweetness than grit.

Nothing brought this out more than being around people. He loved them all, large and small, old and young, requiring only one thing in return for the love, loyalty, and licks he gave—touch.

I used to joke with friends that if someone organized a pet-a-thon and Humphrey was petted for umpteen straight hours, the second you removed your hand from his body, he would begin to whimper. He would go to any lengths for affection.

Soon after Lori enrolled in a certification course to become a massage therapist, she began inviting a group of fellow students over to the house to practice the techniques they had learned. Humphrey would invite himself to the gathering, hopping on the massage table between students and demanding they try a few relaxation techniques on him.

The scenario was no different when Lori and I desired some intimate time alone. Humphrey, always needing to be where the action was, would appear within moments on our bed. He would behave like a little boy when I would usher him outside, barking and whining before eventually accepting our need for privacy.

Constant touch was his preference, but your company was his lifeblood. He simply wanted to be everywhere you were. If you sat on the couch to watch TV, he climbed up to join you. If you sat at the desk to work, he sat beneath you. If you wandered into the living room at 4 A.M. because you couldn't sleep, he followed you. If you had a camera in your hand, he was your subject. Every single time you left Humphrey behind, to run an errand, grab dinner, go to a movie, or whatever, he gave you a look that amounted to *Aren't you forgetting something?* Humphrey's patented guilt gaze was 100 percent effective. If you could possibly take him, you did; if you couldn't, you felt terrible.

Humphrey's need for human intimacy worked well with the homebody lifestyle Lori and I had cultivated. Lori spent much of her free time tending to the garden, which had been left in immaculate condition by an organic farmer who previously owned the property. When I wasn't fixing or fiddling with something around the house, I loved to sit beneath one of the oaks in an Adirondack chair and digest a good book. Neither of us being big fans of TV, we often spent our nights lounging beside a blazing fire.

Besides Lori and me, there was always someone around the house for Humphrey to visit with. His weekly favorite was Halvy the poolsmith, who always gave Humphrey a rousing welcome when he burst into our backyard and talked to him as if he were a close friend for the entire thirty minutes he circled and cleaned our pool. Jack, a shy seven-year-old boy down the street, loved to stop by on the weekends and sit with Humphrey inside the empty old redwood hot tub. Even the gardeners, who were at first startled by Humphrey, soon grew to welcome his constant company as they worked around the yard.

The only humans Humphrey didn't take well to were those who approached our front door in uniform. UPS, FedEx, or the pizza person—it didn't matter what your colors were, Humphrey had a blind compulsion to defend his property from, in his eyes, potential intruders.

Having a pizza delivered illustrated this best. Once Humphrey heard the sound of the driver's wheels roll onto our gravel driveway, he would go bananas. Lori would, after a brief struggle, corral Humphrey and take him to our bedroom in the back of the house. While I paid for the pizza the driver couldn't help but hear Humphrey barking his brains out behind the closed bedroom door. Often the drivers would nervously ask as we performed our transaction, "Are you sure that dog is locked away?"

Once the driver had left and the coast was clear, Lori would let Humphrey out. He would come flying through the living room, slide on the lanolin kitchen floor, and stand on his hind legs to look out the kitchen window for any sign of the driver. He would then sniff out every corner of the kitchen and the area around the front door, which was accessed through the kitchen. It would take him a couple of minutes before he would call off his hunt and begin panting for a slice of pizza.

UPS and FedEx drivers fared no better. When they would see Humphrey barking behind the wrought-iron fence in the front of our property, they would nervously toss the package on our front porch without even making an attempt to see if anyone was home to sign for it. The same went for the mailman, who would toss oversized packages, which didn't fit in our mailbox, in the direction of our front door and scurry away.

There was an eventual truce with the FedEx driver.

One day I caught him outside and asked, "Are you afraid of dogs?" He replied, "Not nice ones." I did my best to explain that Humphrey just needed to be part of everything and if the driver allowed himself to be checked out, Humphrey would silence his harsh greeting. The driver didn't seem overjoyed with my peace offering.

However, not long after I'd broached the idea, the driver agreed to meet Humphrey in the neutral ground of our front porch. I went out back, clipped Humphrey to the leash, and brought him to where the driver was standing. Just to be on the safe side, I held Humphrey with no slack on the leash.

Humphrey performed a canine version of Connect the Smells—first the shoes, then the pants, next the clipboard, straight to the crotch, back over to the package, and onto the hands—without a hint of aggression. When Humphrey finished, the driver slowly leaned down to pet him. As Humphrey licked the driver's hands, he leaned his body into the man's, inviting intimacy. With their differences resolved, the two became a team, as the driver would hand all future packages to Humphrey, who would deposit them (most times) by our back door.

A couple of deliveries later, the driver even let Humphrey onto his truck. Humphrey immediately bolted to the back and began fervently sniffing around as if he had lost an important package. The driver was incredibly patient with Humphrey's unending curiosity. When

Humphrey finally made it back to the front of the truck, the driver was waiting with a large Milk-Bone.

Humphrey's interactions with other dogs were limited to dogs he saw at his training class at the local humane society, dogs that bordered both sides of our property, and dogs he would see on jaunts up Sulphur Mountain Road, a nearby trail that we hiked on weekends. Given his discerning chow personality, the one-dog environment of our sprawling property suited Humphrey just fine.

So I was startled one afternoon to look into our backyard and see Humphrey chasing a young black Lab. He would chase the Lab in long circles around the deck of the swimming pool and the surrounding oak trees before finally catching the dog underneath the orange tree and playfully gnawing its neck while it lay submissively on its back. Then it was the Lab's turn to be "it"—and off they ran.

Lori and I traced Humphrey's unexpected four-legged friend to our new neighbors, who had recently moved in across the street. The Lab's name was Sheeba, and she was just a year old. In the days that followed, she would find her way into our yard in any way possible.

Most times she would use the force of her snout to push open our white-latch gate, which was severely warped from the rain and wouldn't completely close. Her sidekick, Brandy, a mutt of many mixes, would wander over with her, but as soon as Brandy got near, Humphrey would launch into a jealous barking rage that would send her back home.

I was thrilled that Humphrey had found a love interest, and Lori and I got a kick out of watching them play. But both of us had concerns that Humphrey's intensity might prove too much for such a young, less powerful dog.

One lazy Sunday afternoon, after they had been chasing one another for a good twenty minutes, trouble struck. Humphrey was in headlong pursuit of Sheeba when, her legs wobbly from fatigue, Sheeba was unable to propel herself over the three-foot concrete lip that led to the swimming pool deck. She slammed into the concrete ridge and fell to the ground. She didn't get up and she wasn't moving!

Lori, known for her Buddhalike calm in the face of crisis, didn't panic. I was worried about Sheeba but also concerned that her owners, our new neighbors, who were laissez-faire in monitoring her whereabouts, would blame us for her accident.

Lori and I sat on each side of Sheeba and gently stroked her belly and softly spoke to her. Humphrey looked on, concerned and confused. It was several tense minutes before she finally got back up on her four paws. After this incident, we felt it best, at least for a while, to try to seal up the yard so we could better monitor Sheeba's playtime with Humphrey. I went out and fixed the white fence so it would shut tight.

The plan worked well for the first day. But the next afternoon, while I was making lunch, I heard scratching at our front door, which opened off the kitchen. I looked down toward the welcome mat and saw Sheeba looking up at me with the sweetest, most innocent gaze.

Later that day, sitting in my office at the front of the house, I was shocked to hear rumblings coming from the backyard. You guessed it—Sheeba and Humphrey were running wild again. After they played for a bit and it looked like it was getting to be too much for Sheeba, I opened the gate and sent her back home. She looked at Humphrey, then at me, as if she were saying good-bye to a lover going off to war.

The break-in artist struck again and again, day after day, for an entire week. Lori and I were completely mystified as to how Sheeba kept getting into our yard!

I set out on a thorough investigation of all possible entry points to our backyard. I had Humphrey by my side, in hopes that he would tip his paw with some clues (he didn't). Together, we combed the entire acre of our property, but after an exhaustive search, I found nothing suspicious.

I decided to take one more walk down a sliver of space between the east side of our house and a wooden-slat fence that divided our property from our next-door neighbor's. There, midway along the length of the house, I spotted a small hole dug beneath the fence. It was so tiny that I couldn't imagine Sheeba fitting her body through the opening.

The next day, spying from the house, I saw Sheeba in action. I couldn't believe what I was witnessing. The way she shimmied and squirmed her body under the fence and through the small opening was incredible. I was moved by her determination and certainly didn't want her to have to continue making such a painstaking effort to come see Humphrey. From then on, we let Sheeba in the backyard through the gate or the front door.

Thankfully, Sheeba never had any other mishaps while playing with Humphrey. I suppose every love affair takes a spill from time to time.

It's hard to pin down a specific moment or time when Humphrey wiggled his way deep into my heart and made his indelible mark. But I do remember the moment I admitted he had. It was over a summer vacation while visiting Lori's parents on Cape Cod. In casual conversation her father, Lou, politely asked, "How's the dog doing?" My reply was, "Lou, I used to look at people who were crazy about their pets as lunatics. Well, you're now looking at one!"

Sadly, Humphrey's blissful bucolic life, which had defined the first five years of his life, came to an end when Lori and I decided to part ways. Like anything large in scope, there were a lot of little earthquakes that led to my break up with Lori. Thankfully we had no children caught in the middle of our divide, and, all in all, it was a respectful, peaceful parting.

But that didn't mean it wasn't emotional. After all, we shared a dog that we were both incredibly fond of and to whom we were both attached. Lori knew I was nuts about Humphrey and that for a person with my solitary nature, he meant everything to me. And if my world were about to be made smaller by one huge piece, Humphrey would become the center of my universe.

When Lori saw me on the floor tussling with Humphrey, looking more canine than human, she would say, "I get the feeling that if I weren't here, you guys would get along just fine." Still, there had been no mention as to who would take Humphrey on the next leg of his journey.

On a dreary weekend afternoon, the question resolved itself. Lori and I were sitting in the living room having that surreal conversation a couple has after their love has ended and only the logistics of their separation remain. I knew this moment had been building for some time, but the reality of it hit me hard.

As Lori sat with me, trying to provide comfort, Humphrey appeared outside the back door, barking to be let in. Lori got up to open the door and when she did, Humphrey rushed in and sat on the ottoman next to me. With Humphrey beside me, like a security guard protecting something fragile, Lori looked at him, then at me, and said, "You've got your trusted companion—you'll be okay."

That night I had an emotionally charged telephone conversation with my sister, Marcy, about a family issue. I was sitting on the same green sofa chair, with my feet extended onto the ottoman. Humphrey was clear across the large rectangular-shaped living room, lying on the couch.

As the exchange between my sister and me became more heated, Humphrey walked over from his place on the couch, climbed onto the ottoman and draped his body over mine. Most times he would lean up against the side of the chair so I could pet him, occasionally he would hop onto the ottoman, like he had done earlier in the day—but he had never done anything like this before. There he lay, his entire body, except for his hind legs, covering mine. He looked up at me with a stern yet sensitive pout, trying to soothe my anger.

This gesture would be a precursor to Humphrey's new role as my emotional barometer. From Ojai onward every time I raised my voice or got intense in conversation with someone in person or over the phone, Humphrey would begin to growl. If I didn't take his signal to soften my tone, his growl quickly escalated into rapid-fire barking. It only occurred a half-dozen times or so a year, but he never made a false reading: If Humphrey was barking, I was troubled about something. His psychoanalytic skills were far more effective in altering my negative behavior than any shrink had ever been.

I was heading into a tough transition, but I was grateful to be making it with my four-legged soulmate.

Shortly after the conversation with Lori, I put the house on the market, and after three months of searching, found a marketing position with an education software start-up in Northern California.

In a blink of an eye and the wag of a tail, Humphrey and I were on our way to a one-bedroom apartment in Mill Valley, just across the Golden Gate Bridge from San Francisco.

A year had passed since I'd sold the business I'd co-owned with Steve. I had spent the time pursuing photography, a passion I hoped one day would become a career, and looking into new business ideas, none of which had panned out. It was time to get back to work, and I welcomed the inflated dot-com salary and steady cash flow that the upstart company offered. I was also relieved, and somewhat excited, to put the emotions and marital memories of the Ojai house behind me.

But I worried about Humphrey.

How would he handle this major change of lifestyle?

How would he react to a remarkably smaller living space with no backyard after spending most of his life in a pooch's paradise? How would he deal with the close proximity to other people, both within our apartment complex and surrounding it? And how would he deal with the countless daily interactions with other dogs?

I had hired a trainer while we were still in Ojai to give Humphrey some additional obedience lessons, and I knew I had to move on with my life, but, still, I felt like a parent who was failing his child.

George Marshall, the old-timer I had hired to work with Humphrey, had been around dogs since just after they evolved from the wolf. He tried his best to set me straight, saying, "Mark, dogs adjust much better to change than humans. They don't drone on for hours about what is or isn't. If you give them a loving home with good treats and sufficient exercise, their tails will be wagging."

We arrived at our new apartment at 9 P.M., and except for a small light in the kitchen, the place was dark. The movers were to arrive the next day, so the apartment was empty except for a few cable wires dangling from the wall and a couple of Styrofoam cups the cleaning crew must have left behind. Humphrey poked around the apartment, wondering if this was a stopover or our final destination. I pulled out an inflatable bed I had bought on the ride up, and Humphrey and I managed a meager night's sleep in the center of the living room.

I awoke to the stark reality that my marriage and our life in Ojai were over, and I felt desperately empty. I suppose I had good reason, finding myself concurrently embroiled in three of the five most stressful things in life—divorce, moving, and a new job—all at the same time. To add to this, I didn't know a single human where I had just moved or at my new job.

It felt strange to be in our new environment without Lori; the cats, Steinway and Coozer; and our glorious backyard. It was now just Humphrey and me, and I would have to assume new roles in Lori's absence. Unlike in Ojai, where I would open the back door in the morning and let Humphrey play in the yard all day, here in Mill Valley we would be in each other's face and space pretty much the entire time I was home. It was time for us to see each other up close—warts, whiskers, and all.

We compromised and easily settled our few differences.

He liked to get up early, grab a quick breakfast, and pee on something green before I even wanted to open my eyes. I deferred to Humphrey on this one (as if I had a choice), and he gladly became my alarm clock.

Not the kind of alarm clock, mind you, that allowed you to hit the snooze button and buy another five minutes. With Humphrey jumping off and on the bed in excitement, I was lucky most mornings if I could buy five seconds. When jumping on the bed didn't do the trick, he would resort to whining; if whining didn't work, he would begin to bark.

One way or another, I would be standing over a bag of dog food, half asleep at 6:30 A.M., feeding Humphrey breakfast.

Feeding Humphrey had always been Lori's responsibility; now it was mine. Like most dogs, Humphrey always wanted more than the portion I fed him for breakfast and dinner. Firmly believing that a dog's weight was one of the few things in life you could actually control, I fed him 1½ cups of lamb and rice twice a day, which was the recommended amount. But that didn't deter Humphrey from trying, every meal, to use his snout to make me spill more than the intended amount of food into his bowl.

To make up for being an anal owner who faithfully fed his dog no more than the recommended serving, I initiated a lunchtime bone program, which featured the best in canine cuisine. One whiff of kitchen smells, signaling that I had started to prepare my lunch, and Humphrey would position himself just outside the kitchen entrance, paws crossed, anticipating the bone of the day.

And then there were walks. This was a biggie. No matter how far we walked into the recesses of Mt. Tam behind our apartment, Humphrey wanted to go farther. Lack of stamina, and most often, time constraints, didn't garner much empathy from Humphrey. Wherever we were, however far we had traveled, when it came to turning around and heading home, Humphrey opposed the idea. He registered his opinion with one of his many unmistakable facial expressions that left no mystery as to what he wanted. Inevitably, we always went a little farther, and a little farther....

To give Humphrey more exercise, and to socialize him with other dogs, I brought him to a local dog park, a foreign concept while we lived in Ojai. It was amusing to see Humphrey swarmed by ten dogs as soon as he tucked his tail inside the large fenced-in play area. Initially he would be very tense as all those dogs poked around his private parts. But once he got the hang of it, he was fine.

The typical dog activity at a dog park—chasing after round objects thrown by their owners and diligently returning them—was not Humphrey's forte. He would happily comply the first couple of times I would toss a tennis ball, and then lose interest, shooting me a look that said: *Fetch and retrieve, fetch and retrieve, fetch and retrieve—who needs that over and over again? I realize you want to impress your fellow dog owners—'Look at my well-trained dog' —but frankly if I see a tree I'd like to mark, a hole I'd like to dig or a butt I'd like to sniff, you're out of luck.*

Occasionally he would hook up with a dog that he liked and they would play, but most times you could find him walking the perimeter of the park alone, sniffing and watering the greenery. He had been raised in a solitary environment, and when it came to canines, he was friendly, but a bit of a loner.

The worst part of our new arrangement was having to take Humphrey out to relieve himself when it rained. It didn't matter how furiously it was coming down, Humphrey had to find the right spot. And with the rain making it near impossible to use his sense of smell to determine that perfect spot, there would be one frustrated owner and one drenched dog when we finally returned to the apartment. I couldn't blame Humphrey but it didn't stop me from pleading with him to get on with it.

I was slowly making my way into a new life. Professionally I had gone from owning a small business with one partner, where I was surrounded for eight years with primarily the same group of people in a four-room office, to working in a tiny cubicle for someone else, surrounded by an ever-growing group of fresh faces. The corporate culture of endless meetings and an emphasis on strategy versus action, along with a CEO who was burning through the company's coffers with frivolous expenditures was eye-opening, and, at times, exasperating. My saving grace, and what ultimately made the experience worthwhile, was the marketing team, the most talented, zany, and creative group of people I had ever been around.

My first choice had been to work for Pets.com, the then-dominant online pet retailer. I had applied for a marketing position there well before the software start-up opportunity came about. After sending the marketing director a creative direct-mail campaign, I was flown to San Francisco for a Friday afternoon interview.

The company's office space was a dream for dogs and dog owners. Everywhere you looked there was a slew of fun toys and tasty treats. From the reception area, I could see a row of dogs with their heads hanging out of their owners' cubicle spaces. The building, once a tire factory, was now a dot-com refuge, complete with high ceilings, ping-pong tables, and two on-staff masseuses. The place was abuzz with energy, youthful exuberance and poss-ibility. I was drooling to be hired.

I was met in the lobby by Julie, a twenty-something transplant from Dallas, who headed the marketing com-munications department. I hadn't been in a job interview for ten years, but I was amped and ready. I had thoroughly researched the pet industry (online and off), knew pertinent information about the company's marketing strategy, and came armed with a long list of marketing ideas.

In a large back room, with Julie's faithful canine companions, Murphy and Spike, by her side, I answered her questions and pitched my ideas. She stopped me often to praise my creativity and preparedness, and to explain how she had used a similar creative approach when first joining the company. I had, in her words, "Exactly the kind of outside-the-box thinking we are looking for." For the final leg of my interview I met with the head of human resources. After a short but smooth conversation, the woman told me to expect a call the following Monday morning.

Walking out of the interview, I was certain the job was mine. It was just a matter of the formalities.

After not hearing from anyone by late Monday afternoon, I called Julie to follow up. This woman whom I had sat before just seventy-two hours earlier, spewing every creative idea I had had in this lifetime and the previous one, had apparently forgotten who I was! After a few moments of unbearable uneasiness, she coolly acknowledged me and said she or someone in human resources would contact me when a decision had been made. I never received a call.

In the end there was a small measure of satisfaction to the turn of events: the company I ended up working for outlasted the company that had rejected me.

Like most companies, my new place of employment didn't allow dogs at work. So Humphrey entered yet another new world—doggie daycare.

I found a daycare center conveniently located right around the corner from where I worked. Before being accepted as a new camper, Humphrey was given a thorough temperament test by Brent, the owner of the business. As I looked on through a Plexiglas window, Brent led Humphrey through a series of interactions to measure his behavioral responses. He then instructed Gracie, his ten-year-old golden retriever, to administer the "ultimutt" test of canine compatibility. She made a full circle around Humphrey as if she were inspecting a new car for purchase, then pranced on her front paws to initiate play. Humphrey got the lick of approval from Gracie and a couple of bones from Brent for a job well done. While Gracie and Humphrey continued to play, Brent gave me a tour of the facility. It was clean and well organized, with ample indoor and outdoor space for the twenty to thirty dogs that stayed there on a daily basis.

When I picked Humphrey up after his first day, he was completely wiped out. When I got him home, he fell asleep immediately. This was unheard of for Humphrey, and I actually thought, for a minute, that something might have happened to him at the daycare. But it turns out he was simply adjusting to the active, fun-filled curriculum of his new K9-to-5 existence.

I came across additional, unexpected care for Humphrey from a next-door neighbor. Humphrey and I met Carlo, who had just celebrated his seventieth birthday, while he was out walking Pepper, his twelve-year-old husky. It was an endearing sight to watch Carlo help Pepper, who was suffering from debilitated hind legs, up a long, narrow flight of stairs every day after their walk.

As Pepper's quality of life deteriorated more and more, Carlo made the gut-wrenching decision to put Pepper to sleep. Missing Pepper terribly, he would offer to take care of Humphrey every time he saw us on a walk, saying, "If you ever need help with him, please let me know." It wasn't too long before I took him up on his offer. He immediately became a godsend, watching Humphrey whenever I went out of town or visited friends in the city for an extended period of time.

Like all who came to know Humphrey, Carlo got a real kick out of his gregarious personality. When Carlo would open his front door, Humphrey would burst inside and give everything within nose level a once-over. Then he would run into Carlo's bedroom and romp on his bed, before positioning himself in front of the cookie jar in the kitchen. Humphrey loved Carlo's generosity when it came to his bone supply. He had that "grandfather leniency" in indulging Humphrey that I never had, and, of course, Humphrey loved him for it.

Along with the scrumptious goodies and doting attention, Humphrey loved the walks he and Carlo took through idyllic Mill Valley. It was good exercise for Carlo, and Humphrey loved the attention he would get while visiting with Carlo's friends in the town square. When I picked up Humphrey, Carlo would always give me a full report: "We walked, he peed, he pooped. I must tell you, Mark, he was a wonderfully behaved boy."

Every time Humphrey and I would walk past Carlo's place, Humphrey would stop and try to forge his way inside the gate to see his friend. When he would hear Carlo talking to someone on the sidewalk, just below our second-story apartment, Humphrey would whimper, jump up onto the couch next to the window, and bark to get Carlo's attention.

A little over a year after my job began with the software company, our funding, like so many other dot-coms', dried up. It was a harsh ending to a promising beginning.

On the morning of a paycheck Friday, word spread among the employees that the company wouldn't be able to make payroll. Called into the conference room a few hours later, we were told by the CEO that we had, indeed, run out of money. While management scrambled to secure an unlikely bridge loan, it was each employee's decision whether to continue coming into work without pay. I showed up for a couple of days to tie up some ongoing projects, collect my things, and say my good-byes. During those few days, a couple of more bombs dropped— it was discovered that the employees' health insurance premiums were not current (a few employees had pregnant wives at the time), and that the company had not been making contributions to employees' 401(k) plans. Valentine's Day was my last day with the company.

Humphrey took the news well. It meant we would be home together, spending the mornings scouring the online job postings and the afternoons taking extended hikes through the lush landscape of Marin County. Over the next couple of months, the number of marketing positions (the first jobs to be cut in a downturned economy) became less and less, and for every desirable position there were hundreds of resumés (over a thousand in many cases I knew of) flooding human resource departments.

I began to explore other horizons.

The closest I had been to nature as a kid was on family vacations where my dad, playing tour guide as we drove along in the car, would say, "We're not going to go there, but down that road is..." Mine was a family with plenty of drama but very little adventure.

It wasn't until I was thirty-two, when I took a brief trip to Yosemite with my friend, Mike, that I experienced a true wilderness moment. I can vividly recall it. Mike and I were hiking through a meadow when he suddenly re-membered that he had forgotten to call his girlfriend as promised. With Mike back at the camp using the pay phone, I stood alone for the first time among the fragrances, color, and tranquility of nature. In those fifteen minutes while I awaited Mike's return, I discovered a sacred place able to transfer me into a world of bliss and beauty no matter what my state of mind.

When I had moved to Ojai, I developed a voracious

appetite for the outdoor world. I soon discovered the Los Padres National Forest, Ojai's desolate and stunningly beautiful backcountry. As an extension of my appreciation for nature, I bought a Canon SLR-type camera. Every weekend, I would drive up winding Highway 33, park my car in the middle of nowhere, wander through nature, and wait for sunset to paint the landscape with warm, rich tones.

Out of work in Mill Valley, I picked up my Canon again, only this time I was drawn to dogs. My test subject and star, of course, was Humphrey. I snapped countless shots of him at local parks, in outdoor open spaces, and in our apartment. Dogs may not understand the photographic process—that the camera produces a still image of their likeness—but many seem to have a sense of what's taking place and what's required of them. Humphrey was a shutterbug's dream. He was photogenic and played to the camera like few dogs I have photographed.

After a solid month of capturing Humphrey in color and black-and-white, an idea struck me one evening—"what about a photography book on old dogs." The brainstorm was the culmination of several elements: Humphrey was approaching eight, senior status for large breeds; I was struck by the exclusion of older dogs in TV commercials, print ads, and movies; and I felt that older dogs, with their distinguished looks and gentle souls, would result in moving photographic images. It didn't hurt that after doing some research I discovered, among the immense litter of dog books, there was not a single illustrated book on old dogs!

Along with the convergence of these elements, I soon came upon Mollie, an eleven-year-old Irish setter who instantly struck me as a perfect first candidate for my book project. Humphrey and I regularly ran into her and her human counterpart, Jean, after we switched to a different walking route on Mt. Tam. Jean was a strong, independent woman who had what she wanted in life and didn't want to be bothered. She lived at the top of the mountain with her husband, a doctor in town; her children were grown and gone.

During our first several encounters, Jean and I exchanged polite hellos. Mollie, fresh from romping through the streams that ran down Mt. Tam like hot fudge on an ice cream sundae, always greeted Humphrey with whiffs and wags.

One day I told Jean about my idea for a book on older dogs, and expressed my desire to make Mollie part of my project. Jean seemed remotely interested and took my telephone number. I was silent on the subject the next couple of times I saw her. A week later, in a persistent mood, I brought up the possibility, again, of photographing Mollie. Like before, Jean took my number and didn't call. I can't say I was entirely surprised I hadn't heard from her: the fanny pack in which she put my telephone number was a black hole of countless crumpled notes, disheveled dollar bills, and various sundries.

Out of embarrassment or actual interest—I couldn't tell which—Jean stopped me one day and offered a date and time in which I could come by her place to do my photo shoot with Mollie.

Jean's backyard, tucked among towering redwood trees that drizzled diffused light through their limbs, provided ideal light for capturing Mollie. An hour went by in a minute as I followed Mollie from place to place in her environment.

Later in the week, when I brought the developed test prints to Jean and her husband, Jack, I was surprised by their overwhelmingly positive reaction to a particular close-up of Mollie. The photograph was not among my favorites, but, following their enthusiasm, I decided to include it in my pitch to publishers.

Many people who saw my body of work suggested I begin charging dog owners for my portraits (I had not charged any of the dog owners to photograph their dogs for my book project). By this time, the job market was getting worse—the ranks of my unemployed friends and business associates were growing. I certainly preferred the blue skies and fresh air of the outdoors to the drab gray air-conditioned cubicles of office jobs, and relished the thought of working with dogs. And so my pet portraiture business began.

On July 3rd, months after I had submitted my book proposal to publishers, the president from a prominent publishing company called to say he wanted to publish my book on old dogs.

In order to ensure a fall release of the book for the following holiday season, I had only a two-month window in which to turn in my materials—50 photographs of older dogs, plus each dog's "longevity secrets." Humphrey was not the ideal photographer's assistant (to him there was only one subject worth shooting), so I didn't take him on my photo shoots for the book project or my commissioned jobs, but he much preferred the hours of my new career versus my old one.

I never could have dreamed when I first pulled out my camera, after years of inactivity, that my passion for dogs, in combination with my artistic abilities, would result in a career, much less a published book. But that's what happened.

Life was good. I had emotionally come through my divorce and was now dating someone new. I had transitioned in an extremely short period of time from a career as a small-business owner to that of a working artist, a vocation much closer to my calling. And my first book was in the works.

None of it would have been possible without Humphrey. I didn't have much when I first arrived in Mill Valley, but I had Humphrey—excited to check out his new surroundings, meet the new neighbors, and begin another chapter in our life together. No matter the challenges of acclimating to my new life, I knew Humphrey was waiting on the other side of the door when I got home and on the other side of my bed while I sat up sleepless nights trying to sift through the emotions of where I was and where I'd been. Everyone needs a source of light, outside of themselves, to get them through their most difficult times. Humphrey was mine.

Getting back to my life after Humphrey passed away ... With Jeff's family about to return from Mexico, and the stretch between Christmas and New Year's about to make its highly anticipated and, at least for this year, unwelcomed appearance, I decided to go to a place where its presence would be less pronounced.

Years ago I had read an article about a sanctuary for abused and abandoned animals in southwest Utah called Best Friends. As many as 2,000 volunteers passed through each year—many on the way to nearby national parks like Zion and Bryce Canyon—to do their part to help the animals. Some couples had even chosen this animal lover's oasis as the perfect place to get married!

The idea of being around a lot of dogs and pouring out the love I had in my heart for Humphrey seemed like a positive one. Even though I desperately missed Humphrey and the companionship he provided, I knew I wasn't ready for a new dog. Perhaps, I reasoned with myself, Best Friends would be a good intermediary step.

While I wondered if being in a kennel environment would make me think of Humphrey's last hours, I was slowly learning that there was no way around my pain—I had to go through it—and if the road to healing went through a pack of pooches who were in need of love, I was all for it.

My career as a pet photographer would still be there when I had the heart to pick it up again. For now, photographing someone else's pet, having just lost my own, was the last thing on my mind. Thankfully, I was no longer in a service business, like the courier service I had once owned, with a clientele that needed to be served daily to be preserved. I was fortunate that the years I had spent in that endeavor had provided me with enough savings to tide me over until I began working again.

I called Best Friends and spoke with Jean in the volunteer department. She gave me a quick rundown on their program. I would need to partake in a short orientation and tour of the sanctuary before volunteering and I could volunteer for as little or as much time as I wanted so long as I kept her apprised of my schedule. Unlike Southern California, Utah was actually in the midst of winter and had just had a significant snowfall—Jean advised me to "bring warm clothes."

When I got off the phone, I booked a room for a couple of nights at the Shilo Inn, located five minutes from Best Friends. I drafted a note for Jeff's family, thanking them for their hospitality, called my father and a couple of friends, and within a half hour, I was off to Kanab, Utah—home to the largest no-kill animal sanctuary in North America, and the spot Hollywood chose to film *The Lone Ranger*, *Rin Tin Tin*, *Gunsmoke*, and *Billy the Kid*.

Once I got past the traffic-at-any-hour city of Los Angeles, the view was open and inviting—a long, flat stretch of two-lane highway flanked by brown terrain, with snowcapped mountains in the distance. Save for the small roadside towns offering food, gas, and a brief rest, the view remained the same until I approached Las Vegas.

It had been many years since I last traveled in this direction, and the massive checkerboard of housing projects alongside the freeway took me by surprise. Home after home looked exactly alike.

After moving beyond the desert towers of tourism that dot the Las Vegas skyline, I was refreshed by a winding pass of stunning rock formations that stood like giant bookends on each side of me as I passed through St. George, Utah. The mile long stretch was a fitting introduction to the natural beauty that lay ahead.

By the time I reached the final leg of highway that

climbed into Kanab (elevation 4,925) it was pitch black out, with only the occasional oncoming car providing light. I logged the final eighty miles in an autopilot daze, listening to music with the windows cracked to help me stay alert. Habitually, I occasionally glanced into the rearview mirror, looking to find Humphrey, restless in the back cab, curious about our destination and sniffing the cool nighttime air.

Pulling into the Shilo Inn parking lot, eight hours after I began my journey, it looked as if I had the entire motel to myself. The front desk clerk informed me that Kanab shuts down in the winter, with more than half of the stores and restaurants hibernating for the off-season, which stretches into early spring.

Starving, I asked the clerk for a restaurant recommendation. "You can try Houston's," she said.

Thinking of the national steakhouse chain I'd been to in Los Angeles with my father (the meat and potatoes man in the family), I replied, "*Really*, there's a Houston's *here*?"

"Yep, it's just down the road on your right."

I had just driven through the downtown area on the way to the motel and I couldn't imagine I'd missed a Houston's. I was so tired, it actually took me arriving in front of *Kanab's* Houston's for reality to sink in.

Houston's Trails End was a self-proclaimed "cowboy steakhouse." Staring at the building and peering through the window, this place was Western through and through, from its hand-lettered sign atop the roof, to its dark wood interior. *This* Houston's was no trendy city steakhouse—it was the real deal, "where the waitresses wear smiles on their lips and guns on their hips!" My experience ended at the front door, as the restaurant was closed for the winter.

I ended up at Pizza Hut. Accustomed to the walk-up Pizza Huts that are in many airports, I approached the counter to order. After a brief conversation with the young woman behind the counter, I realized that this Pizza Hut still provided old-fashioned table service. I sat down, rested my cold, tired feet and enjoyed a couple of hot slices of pizza.

For dessert, I pulled into Honey's Jubilee, a sixties-style market reminiscent of those from my childhood, with Muzak playing from two large speakers above the entrance. Inside there was a familiar, indescribable odor and off-white linoleum floors. I picked up a Häagen-Dazs ice cream bar out of the door-less freezer that ran the length of an entire aisle and proceeded to the register. I was met there by a sweet older woman who had just come back from a cigarette break: "Is that all, doll?"

Back at the motel I unloaded my belongings from the car. When I opened the door to my room I was pleasantly surprised. The accommodations were simple, clean, and spacious—a steal for the low off-season rate I was paying. I flipped on the wall unit heater to warm up the room and settled into my fourth temporary home in as many weeks.

The next morning, after a continental breakfast which only represented one country, I headed over to Best Friends for the two-hour volunteer orientation. On the way, I got my first daytime glimpse of Kanab.

I took an immediate liking to this one-stoplight town. Its core was typical of a small town that catered to tourism—it had a row of shops filled with knickknacks and memorabilia; a couple of local eateries; a couple of national fast food chains; and the obligatory hospital, city hall, places of religious worship, and library.

But beyond the sound of the hourly church bells that resonated from one end of downtown to the other, the outskirts of Kanab invited exploration, with red-rock mountain ranges and open sky in every direction.

A few miles north of town, I turned off the main road into Angel Canyon, the gateway to the seven sacred sites, noted for their healing energy, and the home of Best Friends. I proceeded past a large horse arena and pulled into the welcome center parking lot. Inside, there was a small group gathered. After our guide, Rebecca, a Southern California transplant, gave a brief welcome speech, we were shown a videotape overview of Best Friends. It was a fascinating story.

The organization was founded in 1980 by a large group of animal lovers from several different countries. At any given time 1,500 furred and feathered residents can be found on the 3,300-acre property. The majority are dogs and cats, but the sanctuary also houses birds, rabbits, horses, pigs, and goats. An annual budget of $14 million—sustained largely through donations from over 250,000 members—goes toward employing a diverse staff of dedicated employees, including executives, administrators, veterinarians, animal care personnel, trainers, and a kitchen staff that produces tasty vegetarian lunches six days a week.

After the videotape ended, we embarked on a tour of the property by van. Rebecca, who years earlier had been drawn to the slower pace Kanab could offer her and her two young children, began asking each person where they were from and what type of pet they had. As I waited for the conversation to turn to me, I wondered whether I should share Humphrey's story. Over the last month every time I had spoken of Humphrey's fate, it not only hurt like hell but inevitably propelled my mind into a vicious cycle of what-ifs.

My friends, a therapist I had started to see, and all the books I had scoured, seemed to subscribe to the theory that the more times you tell your story, the better you'll feel. Conventional wisdom was that talking about what had happened helped in the healing process. Perhaps this was true, but I didn't feel my story was all that conventional, and airing it, which made me feel awful, didn't seem that wise.

One of my fears in opening myself up to people I

didn't know was to have someone judge my role in Humphrey's death without understanding how intensely I had loved and cared for him. When you're extremely fragile, the opinions of others, real or imagined, can be particularly devastating.

I made a split decision to tell Humphrey's story. These were my comrades, I reasoned—if animal lovers couldn't understand, who could? It turned out I made the right choice.

It's hard for most people to find pearls of wisdom when they hear about a tragedy, let alone the right words to say, but this group turned out to be a good support group. Many of them, in turn, shared stories with me about special animals in their lives who had passed on and how they had healed.

The tour wound through the beautiful, desolate roads of Angel Canyon, traveled primarily by people either working or volunteering at Best Friends. The various buildings that made up Best Friends were spread throughout the property, separated, in some cases, by a good mile.

Ironically, in sync with the title of my first book, our first stop was Old Friends—stomping grounds for the senior dogs. These are often the toughest dogs to adopt out, and many of these tender-aged dogs live out their lives here.

The dogs were split between two modern octagon-shaped buildings, with five or so in each of the ten separate runs. The individual runs had sufficient indoor space, with each dog having its own raised bed; two doggie doors led outside to a large fenced area. Prairie Dog, a favorite of one of the staff members, was plopped down on a dog bed placed by the tiny office that doubled as a feeding station. His sweet, soulful eyes and gentle disposition reminded me of all the wonderful old-timers I had photographed not too long ago for my book.

As we walked from run to run, the dogs peered up at us through the black wire cages. They looked lonely and in need of human contact, reminiscent of the faces one sees at a retirement home for aging humans. It was sad to see these sweet animals spending their final days without a home and someone to love them. But that being the case, it seemed there was no better place for them than this one—it was clean, comfortable, and maintained by a staff that satisfied their every whim.

Leaving Old Friends, we drove into Dogtown, the canine nerve center with the largest congregation of dogs and the veterinarian staff headquarters. Several dogs from Dogtown, along with dogs from other sections of the sanctuary, are taken on the weekends to adoption fairs at pet stores and other locations in and around Utah.

From Dogtown we visited the WildCats Village, where some 350 cats spend their days lounging in cushy beds, clawing to their hearts' content on cedar posts, and climbing wooden catwalks that crisscross the 12-foot-high ceilings.

Our last stop was the Bunny House. But it was more like The Big Bunny House—these rabbits were the size of kittens! Incredibly, 187 of them had come from an elderly woman in Las Vegas who didn't know that you could spay and neuter rabbits. Best Friends picked up the bunnies from the woman, housed them in an old dog kennel building, and separated the bunnies into male and female areas.

After the tour ended some people chose to socialize with the animals. Tired and hungry, I tried my luck again in downtown Kanab and stumbled across the Rocking V Cafe, an offbeat place (for Kanab) serving California cuisine and Italian dishes. As I was being led by the hostess to a window table, Neil Young was singing "Old King," an ode to his late dog, Elvis, through the restaurant's stereo speakers. The brick interior, once the home of Kanab's general mercantile, had quirky southwestern touches throughout; the walls were lined with black-and-white photographs of local landscapes. After feasting on a delicious Portobello mushroom sandwich, I was disappointed on my way out to read a note on the door announcing the restaurant, like seemingly all of Kanab's eateries, would be closing for the winter after December 31, just two days away. I was quite certain I had just enjoyed my last piece of focaccia bread for a while.

Back in my motel room, winding down and dozing with the TV on, I was startled to hear the familiar sound of a dog's collar jingling. Apparently the motel allowed dogs, I thought to myself, listening enviously to a couple talk to their dog as they left their room. As the dog with its owners walked past my motel door all I could think of was that old axiom—What you resist, persist.

Earlier, before the tour of the sanctuary, I had quickly swung by the cottages located just above the horse stalls at Best Friends. The cottages appealed to me because they were close to the dogs and, more importantly, all proceeds from staying there went to Best Friends. The front desk gave me a key so I could take a peek at one of the units. Turning the key to the cottage, I was greeted by a guest and her dog, who were preparing to check-out. She invited me inside to take a quick look around. The cottage had a small kitchenette, a large living room with access to a small outside deck, a bedroom with two queen-sized beds, and Spanish tile floors throughout to make pet cleanup easy. It all looked good; too good and too homey. I knew staying there without Humphrey would be too hard.

The next morning, I reported to Dogtown for my first day of duty. Like the day before, I attended an orientation, this one to outline the rules and regulations for handling the dogs. It was impressive to see the thoroughness and care Best Friends took in providing the animals with the best life possible, from the staff all the way down to each volunteer.

After a short video, Robert, our field volunteer coordinator, handed us each a whistle and a name badge. He told us we were free to volunteer in whichever area we wanted but that Old Friends could use the most help.

A group of us caravanned over to Old Friends, where we were met by Michelle, a recent college graduate who had moved from St. Louis to take a job in this town with a population of 4,500, all in the name of canine love.

Michelle described the nature of the work volunteers do (if you could call it work) as "socialization." This essentially meant giving the dogs lots of love, attention, and walks. She quickly rattled off a few logistics about interacting with the dogs and showed us where the leashes were hung and the bones were stored.

Each volunteer headed for a different dog run. I opened the latch to the run marked number four and was swarmed by five jubilant dogs. They may have been seniors—with cloudy eyes, slower gaits, old injuries, and various medical conditions—but they were filled with love and a great need for affection. Their ages ranged from eight to fifteen, although it was difficult to know each dog's history and, therefore, age. Mixed among them were a few younger dogs in need of a calmer environment.

The dogs clamored for my attention—smelling me, licking me, and jumping on me. Other than the brief time I had spent with Faye's two Labradors, I hadn't been around any dogs since Humphrey. The sensation of being smothered by a group of dogs, and the instant connection I felt to Humphrey, split me wide open, and I began to cry.

"It's okay, it's going to be all right," I kept repeating over and over, trying to comfort the dogs as well as myself, while addressing each pooch with a pat on the head. Like with Humphrey, I couldn't give them enough love, and they couldn't receive enough. We would get along just fine.

I took a quick look at the photographs of each dog that lined the outside of the run, and decided to make Vincent, a nine-year-old Airedale mix, the first dog I would walk since Humphrey.

Outside, with the beautiful snow-covered vistas of Kanab shimmering in the background, we set out on a designated trail that looped around a stand of pine trees. It felt strange to be walking a dog again. A little ways down the trail, I closed my eyes and pretended that Humphrey was on the other end of the leash. When I opened them, I was again overcome with emotion and dropped to my knees, sobbing. Vincent patiently stood next to me, waiting for me to compose myself.

One by one, run by run, I took each dog out for a walk around the trail. Before leading them back to their enclosed environments, I sat briefly with each dog at a bench beside the trail to let them enjoy the quiet, the fresh air, and the feeling of being connected to a surrogate owner.

Every dog made sure I complied with a Best Friends ritual of supplying them with a bone or two before putting them back in their runs.

You would think these pack animals would be happy just to be among their own kind (and some were), but the dogs loved taking walks, even though they had ample room in their runs, and they craved human contact. I wondered if the dogs who had spent most or all of their lives at Best Friends were more content in their environment than the ones who had come from a home. Lila, the staff member who had worked at Old Friends the longest, confirmed that they were. Sadly, there were many cases of extremely depressed dogs, like an eleven-year-old German shepherd named Angela, who had just come to Best Friends from a permanent home.

In the late afternoon, after each dog had been walked at least once, I drove to Angels Rest, the Best Friends pet cemetery, along the back side of the property. We had driven past the cemetery on our tour, and Rebecca had mentioned, after hearing about Humphrey, that I might want to honor him there.

Although I had had Humphrey cremated at the vet hospital, I had declined to keep his ashes. If he had passed away in a different manner, leaving me some time to prepare, I probably would have made a different decision. But Humphrey in death, at that moment, had meant nothing to me. I was still clinging to his life.

Tucked against a rock canyon and blanketed in a foot-deep layer of snow, Angels Rest was serene and beautiful in the shadows of the late-afternoon sun. From one end to the other, it was covered with tombstones; touchingly, some were for young people buried next to their pets. Among the tombstones were life-sized statues of pets, inscribed with poems, and countless rows of wind chime stands, each chime bearing a loving message from the animal's owner. Indented in a stone wall that ran the length of the entrance were spaces reserved for ash urns and pet keepsakes.

As I slowly stepped through the thick snow without a soul in sight, stopping to read the sweet sentiments that mirrored my own, listening to wind chimes dancing in the breeze, there could be no more cathartic a place to mourn the loss of Humphrey.

It didn't matter that Humphrey's ashes were not there or that his name was not inscribed on a wind chime; he *was* there, among all the other selfless animals who had brightened the lives of their owners in immeasurable ways.

If for no other reason, Angels Rest was why I came to Best Friends.

That night I had trouble sleeping and awoke at 4:30 in the morning with a throbbing headache. I went outside, into the freezing cold, to grab a bottle of aspirin I had in the glove compartment of my car. Crawling back into bed, it was impossible not to think of Humphrey. For years he had soothed my migraine headaches with his patient petside manner. Sensing my condition, Humphrey would drop his urges to play as quickly as I would pop three Excedrin, and spend an entire day with me in the quiet darkness until my pain passed. There was no better medicine than Humphrey lying beside me with his head resting on my shoulder.

After hours of early morning TV and a successful attempt for more rest, I returned to Old Friends. As I pulled up in my car, the dogs in the run closest to the front of the building charged the fence and began barking in excitement. The first day had been hard on me and extremely emotional, but I was happy to be back among the dogs.

Two runs into walking dogs, a light snow began to fall. A couple of volunteers, one from Boston, the other from Madison, Wisconsin, greeted the white blanket gently covering the terrain with great disdain; a fellow Californian and I welcomed it like kids on Christmas. I finished walking the dogs in the remaining runs in the first building before heading over to the other octagon to check on two dogs that would soon become my personal care cases—Barnaby and Sheena.

Barnaby was a medium-sized mixed-breed dog who had a neurological disorder that resembled Parkinson's disease. His steady trembling made him seem feeble—he was anything but. This dog begged for bones with the best of them, insisting on a treat before and after his walks.

Every day I would carve out a little TLC time for Barnaby. First, I would take him on an extra long walk. He loved nothing more than to be on the leash, heading down the trail, sniffing the earth. When we returned from our walks, I would get down on one knee, hold Barnaby close to me, and give him vigorous scrubs on his tummy. It seemed to minimize his shaking.

Then there was Sheena, a black Lab mix with sad gray circles around her eyes, whom the staff believed was feral. She would not let me approach her at all on my first day. I thought it might be that she didn't like men, which sadly was the case with quite a few dogs I had met in my time. But Michelle, who had worked at Best Friends for three weeks, had also not been able to break through Sheena's shell.

The next day, the scene played out much the same: every time I got near, Sheena would lower her back, tuck her tail, and scoot away from me. When I tried to approach her in the run, she would bolt out the doggie door. When I followed her outside, she would walk along the fence, staying clear of me. I sat leaning against the fence for a good ten minutes, thinking she would eventually get comfortable with my presence. I bribed her with the biggest bone I could find. Nothing seemed to work.

While I continued to walk all of Sheena's runmates,

she suspiciously kept her eyes on me. Every time she was within the sound of my voice, I spoke to her in a hushed, reassuring tone. A couple times when I was interacting with Winnie, the dog with whom Sheena was the most comfortable, she would come a little closer, but she always ducked away just before I could pet her.

I took a break and headed over to Angels Landing, where the sanctuary serves its vegetarian, cafeteria-style lunches. I joined a large group of volunteers at a long table and listened to their hilarious and heartwarming stories of dogs they had taken from Best Friends for sleepovers. I hadn't known that volunteers were permitted to take dogs off the property. The idea intrigued me.

In the midst of breaking a Best Friends record for the most poop scooped in an afternoon, I contemplated candidates for a sleepover. There wasn't a bad choice in the bunch, but Vincent, the first dog I had walked, was at the top of my list.

It was New Year's Eve, and Kanab was a far cry from Times Square. Why not ring in the new year with a sweet-tempered, appreciative Airedale mix?, I thought. While they dropped the ball in the Big Apple, Vincent and I would celebrate with bones, back scratches, and a couple of beers.

I approached a staff member, Kathy, with my plans to take Vincent for an overnight. She knew I had recently lost my dog and enthusiastically agreed, saying, "It'll be good for both of you."

I drove over to Dogtown, where they checked dogs out for sleepovers. Vincent's records reflected that he had only been on a couple of sleepovers, and sadly, Old Friends was the only home he had ever known.

Shortly after Vincent had his dinner, Kathy rounded up a dog bed, a water bowl, and some treats to load into my car. I walked into Vincent's run to tell him the news and got a rousing response (you would have thought he won the lottery—a lifetime supply of bones, of course). Vincent and I met Kathy at the back of my car, where she was waiting to see us off.

Vincent's excitement suddenly vanished as he stared up into the open cab. He refused to jump in.

"He might be a little shy," Kathy noted, as she began to slap the rubber mat on the cab floor, coaxing Vincent to enter.

"Maybe the back of the cab is too high a jump for him," I offered.

But Kathy, who had been around Vincent for three years, assured me it wasn't. She then put a couple of bones inside the cab to entice Vincent—he still wouldn't budge.

It was at that moment I suspected what was behind Vincent's hesitation—the strong spirit of Humphrey, from up above, was barking in protest, *Hey buster, stay out of my space!* Humphrey had never shared me with another dog, and he wasn't about to acquiesce without a fight.

Finally, after more bone bribery and encouragement, Vincent became the first dog to appear in my rearview mirror since the day I dropped Humphrey off at the kennel in Culver City.

We headed off to Subway, which, considering the dearth of dining options, was becoming my regular hangout. The manager, recognizing me, said to me through the drive-thru window, "If you keep coming in here, we'll think you're a Kanaber."

"How do you know I'm a tourist and not a local?" I responded.

"Locals don't order the Veggie Delight."

Back in the motel room, Vincent was curious about my digs and dug his nose into every corner. I set up his bed to make him comfortable, but he preferred mine, and we sat together and watched the local news.

After dinner, I tossed the tennis ball for him to chase from one end of the room to another, the way I used to do with Humphrey in the long hallway of our place in San Francisco. Vincent, like Humphrey, was not much into returning what he chased.

We took a long walk under the clear, star-filled Kanab sky. The streets were amazingly quiet—it was impossible to tell it was New Year's Eve.

When we got back to the room, I gave Vincent a couple of treats and petted him for a while. You could tell he appreciated the company, but he seemed to be wondering how I fit into his life.

I had been told by a staff member that a fellow coworker had taken a serious interest in adopting Vincent several years ago, taking him into her home for quite some time. Ultimately, she decided not to adopt him and he ended up back at Old Friends. You couldn't help but wonder if the time away had stolen some of Vincent's younger, more adoptable years.

It was a shame, because outside of desperately needing a bath and something to remedy his bad breath, he sure was a cute dog. He had a brown and black wiry coat with brushes of white on all four paws and around his snout and chest. He must have lost his tail somewhere along the way—only a small stub remained, and when he tried to wag it, it literally vibrated. He had the demeanor of a dependable friend, the kind that's always calm in a crisis.

When the magical minute rolled around, changing from the old year to the new, Vincent was fast asleep on the corner of the king-sized bed while I watched the ending of *Willie Wonka and the Chocolate Factory*. During the night it was strange to wake up and hear him breathing, or hear his collar jingle, or hear him get up to reposition himself on the bed. It all reminded me of sweet Humphrey, sleeping next to me not so long ago.

In the morning Vincent and I wolfed down breakfast— his, a bowl of dry kibble, mine, a bowl of Raisin Bran from the motel's continental breakfast selection. After a short pee-and-poop walk, I packed up the car and we headed back to Best Friends.

When we arrived, I unclipped Vincent from the leash to reunite him with his buddies. He wasn't too pleased to be back and gave me a defeated look as I closed the gate to his run.

I began to feel guilty for taking Vincent on a sleepover. Was I simply serving my own selfish needs to have his company? What it must be like, I thought to myself, to be a dog. In this case, every time you're taken out for a sleepover, you never know if you're on your way to a new home or a one-night stand. The promise and potential disappointment (if you're not adopted) must be agonizing.

In some ways this is an everyday occurrence for a dog. When their owners leave, dogs never know when they will return. It could be a five-minute errand or an eight-hour workday. Not knowing, dogs wander and sleep, restlessly anticipating their owner's return. They may be a little miffed if their owner stays away too long, but they always greet their human with a hero's welcome.

Clearly, I realized the reason Best Friends allowed sleepovers: It was a chance for a potential adopter to spend some time with the dog without a commitment, but more importantly, it increased the likelihood of a love connection. I suppose I just had to chalk it up as another one of life's imperfect necessities.

Whatever the case, I felt for Vincent. I was not in a position to adopt him, only to temporarily love him. I sat on the bench just outside the building, closed my eyes, and offered a prayer that someone would find room, in their heart and in their home, for Vincent.

I went back a couple of times during the day to check on him. He seemed subdued, lying on his dog bed in the corner. I pulled up a folding chair and gave him a pep talk in the only language he would understand—attention and treats.

Two weeks into my stay, I had begun to develop a daily routine in my Kanab life.

I would wake up each morning at around 8 A.M. After a couple hours of writing I would head over to Best Friends for lunch (at $4, the cheapest and best lunch in Kanab), and then spend the rest of the day with the dogs. When Old Friends closed at 5 P.M., I would take a drive through Kanab, shooting landscape photos of the surrounding wilderness. My nightlife was reserved for more writing time, reading, and a bit of TV—a schedule tailor-made for Kanab after dark.

It was strange to be in a routine where Sunday didn't feel like Sunday, Monday didn't feel like Monday, and Friday didn't feel like Friday. I had to power up my computer or ask someone if I wanted to know what day of the week it was. No lazy Sundays, dreadful Mondays, or frantic Fridays; just one day after another in the wide-open beauty of Kanab.

I had no timeframe for my stay. My father, who was the only person I spoke to during my retreat, repeatedly asked me the same question in our brief conversations: "Are you accomplishing what you set out to accomplish?"

I didn't know what his expectations were for my trip. Certainly a couple of weeks away wasn't going to magically transform me. Grief doesn't have a timetable. It can be likened to a lingering, thick fog that feels like it will never lift. For the first time since Humphrey's death, I was able to see tiny patches of blue sky. For now it was hard to be anywhere, so Kanab was as good a place as any to stay for a while.

The dogs seemed to second that emotion, they were getting accustomed to seeing me regularly. I grew close to them, and in a way, they all began to feel like my dogs. Many, in personality and physical traits, reminded me of Humphrey.

In Maxine, a two-year-old boxer mix, I saw Humphrey's persistence for generating attention and felt him in her incredibly soft coat. In Checkers, a portly Dalmatian, I saw Humphrey's expressive, all-knowing eyes. In Moose, a Chesapeake Bay retriever with a curly coat like a stuffed animal's, I was reminded of Humphrey's tireless desire to play and in Sampson, a ten-year-old collie mix, I saw Humphrey's ever-youthful appearance.

All of these similarities to Humphrey endeared me to

these dogs, but they also made me miss him all over again.

In line for lunch one day at Angels Landing, I met Jennifer and John, a friendly couple that had recently moved to Kanab from Boulder, Colorado. After filling our plates to the brim, we sat together at a nearby table. Both John and Jennifer worked at the sanctuary, he as a member of the small information technology staff, her among the horses, pigs, and goats.

Having seen me day after day in the dining room, Jennifer and John were curious about what had brought me to the sanctuary and how long I planned on staying. After talking a bit about Humphrey, I turned to Jennifer, the more talkative of the two, and asked how she liked working at Best Friends. "The work I do here is real. Every previous job I've had sucked the soul out of me. Plus, look at this place—it's beautiful," she replied. Looking out the wall-to-wall window at a postcard view of Kanab, eye-level with the mountains in the distance, beneath a beaming blue sky, I nodded in agreement. As I finished eating and was preparing to leave, Jennifer mentioned that one of the pot-bellied pigs where she worked had just given birth to three piglets. She extended an invitation for me to come over and see them and perhaps take a few photographs.

In the late afternoon I decided to pay Jennifer and the pigs a visit. When I arrived, the only person around was Frank, an accommodating man with weathered skin, presumably from a life spent outdoors, and a fixed, friendly grin with as many teeth missing as present.

He informed me that Jennifer had left to run a couple of errands but that he would be happy to show me around. He led me through a barn door and into a tiny hay-bale igloo. Inside, beneath several heat lamps that hung from the ceiling, a mother pig was nursing her babies in the red fluorescent light.

Frank had an incredible reverence and love for animals. He had tons of stories about the animals he'd cared for and his life in general. If you were listening, he was talking.

With Frank squatting in the corner of the igloo, I lay down in the entrance to the igloo and took out my camera. I must have been no more than three feet from the mother pig's nose. She let out a grunt that didn't sound welcoming, and I turned to Frank for translation.

"She's just protectin' her babies, like any good mother would."

I continued to work within the close quarters, as Frank tried to bring the piglets out from behind their mother. He was able to bring them out a little ways, and I got off a couple of frames. Still looking through the viewfinder of the camera, I could feel the weight of Frank's stare on me.

"Hey, I've seen you before," he blurted out with enthusiasm.

"Really?" I said, somewhat startled. "I've been here for about two weeks—maybe you've seen me at Angels Landing at lunch?"

"No, you're that guy from the morning news show on NBC...what's his name?"

Having heard this comparison often over the last few months, as both my and my likeness's hairlines had gone south, I helped him out: "Are you talking about Matt Lauer?"

"Yeah, that's the guy."

"Frank, if I were Matt Lauer, would I be lying down in a hay-bale igloo, trying to get a couple pictures of piglets?"

Next, Frank took me over to see the goats. There were four of them—two males and two females—in a small run with a miniature wooden house in the center.

The star of the show was Snoopy, a two-year-old male that had been raised since birth by humans. Appropriately named, he behaved exactly like a dog. Once I stepped inside the run, he stepped forward to greet me. His fur was as soft as a dog's, and he had two cute wattles dangling from his neck. He even had on a dog collar with a bone-shaped tag attached.

When I pulled out my camera, Snoopy took it as a signal to play. For a goat, I learned, this means ramming you with their horns. Great fun, to be sure, but not well suited to a camera lens. Every time I looked through the viewfinder, there was Snoopy getting closer and closer.

When Frank and I left the run, Snoopy snuck out behind us. Frank didn't see a problem with letting Snoopy sniff around outside the front of the staff offices. Following him with my camera in hopes of getting a couple of decent shots, I was startled to see Snoopy leap onto the hood of one of the parked cars! Laughing heartily, Frank picked up the fifty-pound Curious George of Goats and put him back in his run.

I had heard rave reviews about Zion National Park, just forty-five minutes from Kanab, from several of the volunteers and staff members. The next morning I decided to take a drive and spend the day there. In no time, the deserted, two-lane highway led me to the east entrance of the park.

Arriving in Zion during the off-season is like being on a short guest list to visit paradise. The place was practically empty of people and breathtakingly beautiful—dominated by monolithic red sandstone cliffs, regally accented with snow-crowned tops.

One of the park rangers told me that during the peak season, they close the Zion Canyon scenic route (containing some of the most dramatic views of the park) to all through-traffic except shuttle buses. I may have seen fifty cars, tops, while I was in the park.

I did witness, however, a minor traffic jam along the scenic route when a flock of turkeys decided to take a stroll right smack down the middle of it. Watching from the side of the road, I found it hysterical; many of the motorists found it frustrating. No matter how incessantly they honked their horns or tried to wave the turkeys away, the proud birds continued to mosey along the road.

When the turkeys finally yielded and the cars were able to slowly nudge by them, the turkeys looked up at the motorists, and yelped loudly, as if to say, *Hey you, our kind was here before this road was even built.*

I got a feel for the park, driving from one end to the other, taking in its high points, literally—Checkerboard Mesa (6,670 feet), The Sentinel (7,157 feet), Abraham (6,890 feet), and The Great White Throne (6,744 feet). I then parked my car and wandered through stone alleyways and ascending, narrow trails, which rewarded me with panoramic views of Zion's grandeur. After devouring the environment and shooting off two rolls, I decided to end my day by taking a walk along the Virgin River.

With rock formations towering above me on each side, and the sound of the Virgin River meandering downstream beside me, I was in heaven.

A mile or so down the path, I came upon a group of ten mule deer grazing on some vegetation a couple feet off to my right. Without my camera, which seemed to scare them off, it was much easier to get near them. There were seven females, two adult males, and a young male just beginning to sprout horns.

While the females milled around and chewed grass, the two adult males began to playfully ram each other with their horns. As the deer slowly moved along; I moved with them. The male deer occasionally glanced over at me, but they seemed to be comfortable with my presence. It was the closest I had ever been to deer; never before had I been able to blend into nature and simply observe them. I followed them along for another thirty yards before heading back to my car.

A curse may have brought me to Utah, but it was a blessing being here at this time of year.

As I left Zion and entered Springdale, the southern gateway to the park, I spotted, out my driver's side window, a picture-perfect sunset cast upon a towering plateau. I made a hard right off the road, pulled a few feet into the entrance of an empty amphitheatre parking lot, left my car, and quickly climbed up a small hill to get a better look. Breathless from my burst of energy and the scenery, I finished off my last roll of film and headed back to my car.

Twenty yards ahead of me another tourist was standing with a tiny disposable camera, capturing the same shot, at what I thought was an inferior angle, with not enough remaining daylight. Putting down his camera, as I walked by him, he said, "Beautiful...did you see it?" I gave him a confirming nod, and continued walking. But I didn't exactly know what he meant by *it*, so I decided, a few feet later, to turn and look again at the landscape. To my surprise, a massive full moon was rising between two jagged edges atop the towering cliffs.

Remember: Always save one last shot—you never know what you're going to see on the way back to the car.

I devoured a vegetarian burger, on the largest bun I've ever seen, at Oscar's, an eclectic restaurant with jalapeño Christmas lights and a mirror ball hanging from the ceiling. After traversing the main road back through Zion on my way to Kanab, I impulsively headed north on Highway 89 in the direction of the sign marked "Bryce Canyon." I arrived just before 9 P.M. and grabbed a $40 room at the Ruby Inn, just outside the park.

I woke up early the next morning and arrived at the entrance to Bryce just as it was opening. At twice the elevation of Zion, Bryce was cold and heavily covered in snow from a recent storm. As I drove the flat road that meanders to a cul-de-sac at the park's end, a stiff wind was wrestling through the Ponderosa pines, making a sound like the ocean's roar. I headed down several detour roads that branched off to my left and led to dramatic lookout points showcasing the park's best views.

In Zion I had spent my time staring up at the stunning rock cathedrals; in Bryce, which lies at the edge of a plateau, the most spectacular scenery is found in the canyon below, where mounds of limestones, sandstones, and mudstones have been sculpted by erosion into whimsical shapes called hoodoos. The spiral maze of hoodoos, changing in color with the mood of the light, resembled rock icicles standing upright.

After spending most of the day viewing the park from its plateau, I parked my car at Sunrise Point and descended down a marked trail toward the canyon floor. I explored the sandcastle of rocks like a child on a jungle gym, walking through stone tunnels and climbing on boulders. Having left enough time to get back up the trail before nightfall, I turned back.

As I did, I found myself at the foot of a spectacular rock formation with two stone "windows," vertically aligned, toward its top right corner. The soft rays of sunset were wrapping around the rock like a warm blanket, with slivers of light peeking through its openings. I shot off a few frames, put down my camera, and wiped my brow. The wind had died down and the air was still. A group of hikers I had seen on my way down the trail had moved on. A tiny bird was flitting about, playing peek-a-boo through the holes in the rock. I sat on the ground and watched the day dissolve into darkness.

When I made it back to the Shilo Inn in Kanab, two hours later, I was exhausted. I requested my home away from home, room 122. I slept for ten hours, the longest period since my senior year in high school. After updating my journal with my jaunt to the national parks, I put on my doggie duds: an old pair of army pants seriously soiled from smothering canines, and a fresh T-shirt, and headed off to Best Friends.

I got to Angels Landing minutes before they stopped serving lunch. Wandering to a nearby table with a plate filled with vegetarian enchiladas, salad, and a couple of chocolate chip cookies, I glanced at the available dog for adoption, whose picture, beneath the glass tabletop, I was about to cover. I did a double take—I couldn't believe the dog's resemblance to Humphrey. According to the description below the color photo, the dog's name was Bodacious. He appeared to be a mixed breed of some sort, with perhaps some German shepherd in him.

I finished eating and drove over to Dogtown to check out Bodacious. The woman at the front desk directed me to the area behind the main building where a staff member would introduce me to him.

A whole other world existed behind Dogtown. There were rows and rows of runs widely spread across a sloping hillside, separated by chain-link fences. The dogs with the most severe behavioral problems lived here. Each dog wore a color-coded collar to denote its behavior and thus its approachability. Dogs with red collars were not to be handled by volunteers; dogs with green collars were okay for socialization. I walked up the dirt path, setting off an ear-splitting chain reaction of barking dogs.

A quarter-mile up the hill I was met by Doug, a staff member, in front of the run Bodacious called home. Doug was holding a file on Bodacious and shared a little of his background with me. The records indicated Bodacious was a retriever mix. The first family that owned him gave him up because he ate too much. Wow, someone would actually give up a dog because he ate too much? Imagine how many humans we would give up if the same criteria applied!

A second family adopted Bo, but they "didn't take to him," and decided to leave him in the Arizona desert. Luckily, Bodacious had been found and brought to Best Friends.

Doug asked me about my interest in Bodacious and I told him what had happened to Humphrey and how similar the two of them were in appearance. Doug mentioned that in the two and a half years he'd worked at Best Friends, six dogs had gotten stomach bloat. The dogs in which they were able to detect a problem during the daytime hours were immediately rushed to the on-site vet, operated on, and saved. The ones that suffered at night were found dead in the morning.

Doug went inside the run, secured a leash to Bo's green collar, and handed him off to me. Bo was all systems go—eyes darting every which way, body quivering with excitement, nose clamoring for virgin scents. Doug quickly suggested a couple of different trails we could take, and we were off.

Bo not only had Humphrey's physical likeness and his sensibilities, he acted exactly like Humphrey had as a pup. He was pulling hard, crossing in front of me from left to right and back again like a racehorse with no track or finish line. He marked his territory every two steps, then stopped to dig his paws into the ground, flicking red dirt and snow behind him. Every time I stopped and tried to calm Bo down, he would jump up onto me. It gave me an appreciation of just how obedient Humphrey had become in the last half of his life.

Doug assured me that Bo would calm down once we got away from the commotion of the dog runs, but his spastic energy pulled me for the entire forty-five-minute climb to a summit overlooking Kanab. Perhaps Bo knew something about the view that awaited us—Kanab from above was breathtaking.

The sky was pregnant with a single, huge billowy cloud that cast a dramatic shadow across the valley floor. In between the sea of green trees, the snow was beginning to melt and sink beneath the red clay earth. The air was dead silent, save for the sound of a large bird gliding across our view, cutting the stillness with the swoosh of its wings. It was like being on top of the world with not a soul in it.

I took a few deep breaths, taking it all in, before looking down to see how Bo was doing. I reached down to pet him and he jumped up again, this time resting his front paws on my sweatshirt. He was panting heavily, and with his tongue hanging out, as if a doctor had just instructed him to say *ahhh*, I noticed dark purple spots, a characteristic of a chow. Clearly, there was more of Bo in Humphrey than I had first thought.

With a banana moon hanging in the eastern sky, and the light of day beginning to fade, we headed back down the hill. Bo was slightly tamer on our return trip, and on a level portion of the mountainside I took the opportunity to do some obedience training. We worked on heeling and sitting. Bo rewarded my efforts with a staggered pull and a partial squat.

When we arrived back at Bo's run, Doug was talking to another staff member. They asked me how it went, which I interpreted as, "What do you think about adopting Bo?"

Over the course of my time at Best Friends I had definitely turned a corner in dealing with Humphrey's death. Still, I was far from ready to take on a new dog. Early on, when the pain of losing Humphrey had completely overwhelmed me, I felt that getting another dog was the only way to fill the hole in my heart. Somehow, for better or worse, I was able to get past these moments. I didn't feel I was torturing myself or depriving myself of the joy that a new dog would bring, I just felt it wouldn't be fair to a new dog or myself if I still had unresolved feelings about Humphrey's death.

Back among my fellow volunteers at Old Friends, I

doubled up, taking two compatible dogs out at the same time in order to have enough time before the sanctuary closed to visit with my friends Barnaby and Sheena.

Barnaby was on a walk with another volunteer, so I went to see Sheena. When I entered her run she got up from a lying position and slipped out the doggie door, conveniently located next to her dog bed. I said hello to a few of the other dogs before walking to the outside of the run. As soon as I walked out, Sheena walked back inside.

I took my mind off my failed attempt to reach Sheena by throwing the ball to Winnie in the outside area of the run. A few minutes later, as I casually passed through the inside of the run to leave, I was miraculously able to latch onto Sheena's collar and slowly bring her close to me. Gently cradling her head, I rubbed the sides of her face with soft repetitive strokes. She was still nervous as I softly spoke to her, but I sensed she welcomed the affection.

I hadn't seen anyone, staff or volunteer, attempt to walk her, so I thought I'd try. She allowed me to clip the leash to her collar and was fine leaving the run, but once we got outside, she wouldn't budge. Not wanting to force her beyond her comfort zone, I returned her to her run.

I was disappointed I wasn't able to walk Sheena farther, but I was happy for the progress we had made. I left her with a kiss on the snout and a bone, which she gingerly enjoyed.

It felt good to be making a small difference in the lives

of these dogs. Most had endured difficult circumstances—some had been tied to the gate of Best Friends overnight, abandoned by their owners. Others had been turned in by families who could no longer keep them for one reason or another or by owners who were in ill health. By comforting the dogs and soothing whatever fear and loneliness they had, I felt in some way I was comforting Humphrey in the last hours of his life, which I still hadn't forgiven myself for missing.

Three weeks had passed since I arrived in Kanab. With the passage of time, home—with its obligations, bills, and career pressure—was beckoning. I didn't want to answer the call. I was enjoying the simplicity and solitude of Kanab life and treasured the everyday interaction with the dogs at Best Friends. It was easy to imagine a permanent life here with affordable housing, clean air, and down-to-earth people, surrounded by natural beauty.

I wasn't alone in my affection for Kanab. Over the course of my time at the sanctuary many volunteers I had gotten to know fantasized about pulling up from where they lived and finding a job at Best Friends. Despite the dreary economy, which was still shaking off a dot-com cold, Best Friends was in a growth period and hiring. Many of the employees I met at Best Friends had only worked there for a short time. Each acknowledged that the transition to small-town life had been a major one, but they all seemed happy with their choice.

But for me, Kanab had served its purpose. The dogs and the natural environment had brought me back to life, literally. While initially reminding me of what I had lost, the dogs ultimately had reminded me of one of the things I derive great pleasure from—a pure connection to these extraordinary beings which, unlike with many of our human counterparts, deepens with the passage of time.

On my last day of volunteering I said good-bye to the dogs, presenting each with the largest bone I could find in the bin and thanking them for being a huge part of my healing process. I put aside a special last meeting with Sheena and Barnaby. Sheena was still timid when I approached her, but I was able to give her a last bit of love. Barnaby was Barnaby—appreciative of the touch and treats but always hungry for a little more. The emotion in closing the latch to the last run was as powerful as the feeling I had had saying hello to the first dogs three weeks earlier.

I had promised the staff members at Old Friends I'd tell them when my last day was, but I knew I wouldn't follow through. I've never been much good at good-byes and over the course of my life I've become an expert at slipping away rather than going through a formal farewell. I got into my car and drove away.

As I passed the wooden Old Friends entrance sign on the side of the road, with its illustration of two old dogs leaning on canes, I broke down. Thoughts of Humphrey came flooding back to me. How blessed I was that he had exposed me to the wonderful world of dogs and the immeasurable joy that comes from their company. For the first time I cried for the gifts Humphrey had given me as opposed to the tragic way he had left me.

Back at Jeff's—this time with his family present—I immediately tackled my top priority—finding a place to live. Over the Thanksgiving holiday, during which Humphrey had passed away, I had been leaning toward moving back home to Southern California and had checked out a couple of apartments. But finding one in Los Angeles that fit my criteria—dog-friendly, in a quiet, uncongested area, with a patch of green nearby—seemed like a tall order.

Even though I no longer had Humphrey, I still wanted to find a place that allowed dogs. I decided to sign up for an online rental service that would narrow down the choices of available apartments based on my criteria. I was amazed by how slim my search results became once I selected "dog" on the electronic submission form. Apparently apartment owners, who traditionally don't like to rent to dog owners, remained unchanged in their sentiments despite a significantly downturned economy.

My first week of searching proved fruitless. Every place

I called on or visited was overpriced and tiny. Whenever the person showing me a particular unit would throw out the obligatory, "So, what do you think?", I'd reply, "If beds could fly I'd be fine, if not, I'd be cramped for space."

You couldn't help but think that the few places that *do* allow dogs know they have you over a barrel with the scarce selection that's available to dog owners.

Time was starting to get tight—in a week my lease in San Francisco would expire. I started to ponder the idea that I might be forced to put my stuff in storage until I could figure something out.

In my frustration I dreamed of building my own apartment complex—one that only allowed tenants with dogs. "No dog? I'm sorry, sir, we won't be able to rent that apartment to you. I can, however, give you directions to the local animal shelter—they have plenty of wonderful dogs there in need of good homes."

Inside my imagined Alpha Dog Apartment community there would be two pools: one for humans, and the other, a lap pool for dogs. Next to the small exercise room (you know the ones...that comfortably fit one and a half persons), there would be a doggie daycare center. A dog run would encircle the entire facility, with one side for big dogs and the other for small dogs. The common-area walkways would be lined with poop scoop bags and bone dispensers. If there were enough demand for it, why I might even consider an on-site veterinarian.

The Gods of Relocation must have sensed my frustration. The next day, on a casual drive to the outskirts of Los Angeles, I stumbled upon an enticing building in an open, quiet suburb. The building was not on my list of dog-friendly apartments generated from the rental service, but I thought I'd give it a try. Inside, the leasing agent informed me that, in addition to having no vacancies, his property did not allow dogs. He was able, however, to recommend a similar building, a few miles away, that did.

Two freeway exits later, I arrived at the apartment complex the leasing agent had referred me to. Before entering the leasing office, situated next to a gated swimming pool, I took a quick look around. The place looked promising. The complex was surrounded by homes (quiet); bordered by a creek (nature); and just around the corner from a large dog-friendly park with two baseball diamonds (green). The apartments themselves were grouped into twelve-unit, two-story buildings that closely resembled condominium living with separate entryways for each unit and ample breathing room between the apartments as well as the buildings.

Chellie, the complex manager, a cigarette-smoking, straight-talking woman who passed for a female Rodney Dangerfield, informed me she only had one available one-bedroom unit.

The unit was located on the creek side of the complex, in the shade of a huge oak tree. It was roomy and bright, with all new appliances, including a small washer/dryer unit conveniently tucked inside a closet off the kitchen, and a cushy new carpet in the living room and bedroom. Next to the small dining area, a sliding glass door led to a large deck with views of the creek and the nearby mountains. It seemed quiet, especially for a Saturday. I took one walk-through and said, "I'll take it."

It turns out that Chellie, who lived in the complex with Pumpkin, her three-year-old boxer, was a dog fanatic. She had worked for the property management company that owned the complex for many years and, in the process of a few transfers, had made all of *her* buildings dog-friendly. Each day, she baked a fresh batch of treats for the dogs and placed them in a bowl on the desk opposite hers. While I filled out some paperwork and handed her a $100 check to hold the apartment, a steady stream of dogs and their owners (25 percent of the tenants owned dogs) stopped by for their daily treats.

Back in my car, from my cell phone, I called my friends Fabian and Melissa in San Francisco, to tell them I had found a new place and that I was heading their way, at last, to vacate my apartment. Sensing I still couldn't bear being in my place alone, Fabian offered me their fold-out futon couch for a few nights and a hand in helping me pack up my stuff.

The following morning I headed north, taking the longer, scenic route to San Francisco. Halfway into my drive, I came upon the small town of Templeton. Off to the right side of the freeway a large patch of grass sparked a memory of Humphrey.

A half year ago, I had taken Humphrey with me on a working day trip to Santa Barbara. On our drive back to San Francisco, I had spotted the field and pulled off the freeway to take a look. It turned out to be a high school football field under construction—the goal posts had been erected and the grass had been laid, but the stands and surrounding structures had not yet been built.

The field was detached from the rest of the high school, and as far as I could see, there was nobody around except for a small group of cheerleaders practicing a couple hundred yards away. I parked my car parallel to what would soon become the twenty-yard line and walked Humphrey on the leash to the farthest end zone. With the coast clear, I let him off the leash and we raced like a couple of ten-year-olds from one end of the field to the other.

At the time my little detour with Humphrey was nothing more than a nice break during a long drive, but now the memory of it made me smile. It's funny how we never know which moments will become cherished memories. I suppose that's why we should live each one fully.

I had a strange, uneasy feeling driving through the streets of San Francisco, navigating my way through thick traffic to reach Fabian and Melissa's small apartment two blocks from Golden Gate Park. Just after I entered their apartment, hugged my hellos, and dropped my backpack, the two of them were off to a movie. They extended an invitation, but, beat tired, I opted for visiting with their cat, Nippy, and enjoying a good book.

The next morning, Fabian and I headed over to my apartment. We drove around for a good ten minutes in Russian Hill, one of San Francisco's notoriously difficult places to park, before finally finding a spot to rest our weary wheels. On our three-block walk to the apartment, I saw a couple of dogs and their owners whom Humphrey and I used to see frequently at the park.

I began to get nervous as we got closer to my building. I hadn't been inside in over two months. As I climbed the steep stairs to the top floor, my heart and mind were racing—*What if this whole thing never happened? What if it's all just a cruel joke that's finally ending? What if Humphrey is on the other side of the door I'm about to open?*

What a reunion it would be. Tears, bones, wrestling, belly pets—pure elation. It would be like winning the Super Bowl, the World Series, the NBA World Championship, and the Stanley Cup all in the same moment.

After our celebration, I'd take a long walk straight down Green Street and I wouldn't stop walking until Humphrey grew tired or my knees fell off. Unable to sleep, at about 2 A.M., we would get in the car and drive to Kanab and grab a room at the Shilo Inn. When the sun came up, I'd take Humphrey to Best Friends to meet Vincent, Barnaby, Sheena, Winnie, and the gang.

If only it weren't all in my head....

The inside of my place was dusty and lifeless. As a favor to me, Fabian had come to the apartment after Humphrey had passed away to remove some of the things he knew would tear me apart, but many still remained. Pictures of Humphrey tucked away in the back of a drawer, a tennis ball under the armoire; his black nylon collar, hanging on a wall rack by the front door; a small tear in a bed sheet from his overzealous paws—they all proclaimed, *Humphrey was here*. Each made me sad, but, in a bittersweet way, they were among the only remaining physical remnants of Humphrey, and I was glad to be reunited with them.

Moving about, packing, and organizing my stuff, I couldn't help but feel Humphrey's presence. When I looked at the green sofa chair beneath the bay window, where he used to sit while I worked, I saw Humphrey— sun splashed across his brown fur; eyes halfway closed in a meditative gaze, tongue out; body vibrating like a motor idling. When I walked down the hallway, I felt him rushing by me in hot pursuit of a tennis ball. While I packed up the bathroom, I glanced out and saw him lying alongside the front door, praying I was not preparing to leave. Putting away the couch pillows, I felt him lying next to me with his head resting on my shoulder. Closing my eyes, I could hear him howling at the sound of an approaching fire engine.

I just couldn't help but think somehow, around some corner, Humphrey would appear.

I had long dreaded returning to the apartment and now that I was finally here, I faced a strange dichotomy— on one hand I couldn't wait to pack up and be gone; on the other, I was reflective, remembering the last moments I had shared with Humphrey. Still, I was thankful that I had listened to myself and not gone back to live in the apartment without Humphrey, even for only one night.

I did my best to get everything boxed and ready to be moved. At about 6 P.M., with the apartment losing natural light, I suggested to Fabian that we break and come back the next day. Inside that apartment was the last place I wanted to be when darkness fell.

The next day proved far less emotional and exhausting and we finished the whole job by 10 A.M. With Fabian behind me, I closed the apartment door and secured the top lock.

Endings never happen how, where, and when we dream they will. Like every part of life, endings are a mystery. I learned that lesson with my business partner, Steve. At our most stressful time in owning the business, when we were close to burnout, we would often speculate how it would all come to a close. Would we both sell?

Would one stay and the other leave? If so, which one? Two imaginative minds, we covered the gamut of possibilities, but we never came close to what would actually occur. The closing chapter in Humphrey's life was much the same.

With my belongings packed and a move date set, I had a couple days to say good-bye to Northern California. First, I had to take care of some business. While I was in Utah, a couple from Fairfax, a town up the road from Mill Valley, had contacted me about getting a portrait done of the two of them and Palmer, their two-year-old Lab mix.

Rusty from my time off and slightly slow at the shutter, I was happy to be working again. We hiked up one of the countless outdoor jewels of Marin County and had a great time. Palmer, of course, was the main source of my attention once I put down the camera and rested on the hillside. He was a rescue dog from an organization I knew of from my book project and an inquisitive delight.

On my way back to Fabian and Melissa's in the city, I decided to get off the freeway and take a drive by my old place in Mill Valley. I parked the car and walked the same route Humphrey and I had taken countless times, up the winding roads into paradise.

Coming back down the hill, I stopped by the library to check my email. Inside the entrance, I ran into Jean, the proud mom of Mollie, the Irish setter I had photographed for my book.

"I was going to send you a note," Jean blurted out before saying hello.

I thought perhaps Jean had heard about Humphrey from someone in town and had intended to send me her condolences.

"We had to put Mollie down two weeks ago," Jean said, near tears. "We used the wonderful photograph of her that you had taken to announce her passing."

I then told her about Humphrey. She was shocked, reconfirming with me his age then offering her heartfelt sympathy. It didn't seem that long ago that our paths had crossed every day, Mollie by her side, Humphrey by mine. Who would have thought that Mollie would not only spark my idea for a book on old dogs but that she would become its cover girl? And that now, a little over a year later, both Mollie and Humphrey would be gone, romping together on another plain.

I spent my last day with Fabian and Melissa, visiting old friends and playing tourist, before ending up at a favorite downtown pub and reminiscing about the early days of my friendship with Fabian when we worked together for the software start-up.

The most meaningful friendships I've formed in my life all began when I was six years old and, incredibly, they've lasted to this day. Fabian was the first real male friend I had made in a long time, and I would sorely miss the tandem of our sharp wits and our photographic jaunts through a city rich with diverse, if not bizarre, characters. Both he and Melissa had been incredibly supportive of me both before and after Humphrey's death. No matter how profusely I thanked them, it would never be enough.

Staring out the pub window with a three-beer buzz, I couldn't believe that in less than twenty-four hours movers would drop my life into a new spot. Whether I was ready or not, time was pulling me into a new chapter. I had allowed myself the time to reflect, wander, and grieve; now it was time to move on.

I spent another couple days at Jeff's house taking care of odds and ends while waiting for my moving day. When it came, I drove to my new apartment a half hour before the movers were scheduled to arrive and sat beneath the umbrella oak tree just outside my unit. Staring into the creek below, I thought about Humphrey and how much he would have loved this place: the close proximity to the park; the surrounding rolling hills, teeming with trails; a balcony from which to gaze at the mountains and watch the birds in flight; and a bunch of canine playmates. I had been trying hard to provide Humphrey a life similar to the one he had enjoyed in Ojai; I only wished he had lived long enough to enjoy it.

Within an hour the storm of my personal belongings

hit and boxes were scattered throughout the apartment. Normally a dreadful experience, unpacking the boxes presented me with an immediate task and a place to begin. I dove into organizing my new living space.

The first night I stayed up until 3 A.M. making sure one of my lifelines to the outside world—my computer—was in working order. Each day that followed I worked early mornings into early evenings, moving closer to a setup that constituted home. But the more I put away and the more settled I became, the more I felt an eerie stillness pervade the apartment. Surrounded by the familiar trappings of my old life but feeling the absence of Humphrey, close friends, Best Friends, motel rooms, and scenic panoramas, I sank into a depression.

The next two weeks were among the hardest I had faced since Humphrey's death.

Sleeping in my own bed for the first time and not on a friend's couch or in a motel room, I felt profoundly alone. I missed Humphrey's solid presence on the other end of the bed. On the most difficult of days, I could always count on the sound of Humphrey's paws scrambling against the wood floor in a high-jumpers launch, landing him on the bed and providing my dampened spirits with a jolt of joy. He had been doing it ever since accepting an upgrade from his dog bed, the first night Lori left the house after our split.

I even longed for the battles we used to have jostling

for sleep position. Humphrey would always insist on sleeping curled up right next to my head. For a long time the arrangement was suitable, but eventually I grew tired of waking up with a stiff neck and my body crammed against the wall, with my pillow as much Humphrey's as mine.

I was able to successfully persuade Humphrey to fall asleep elsewhere on the bed, only to wake in the middle of the night and find him right back beside my head. When I would try, in a groggy, blurry-eyed state, to pry him from his place, his seventy pounds would resist and grunt in protest. The only way to get Humphrey to budge was for me to get up, grab a bone from the pantry, and put it at the edge of the bed.

The mornings in my new place were especially tough. From the second I opened my eyes, I felt disoriented without Humphrey. It felt as if I was losing him over and over again with each sunrise.

The A.M. hours would linger like a stagnant dark cloud. Day after day I looked at what needed to be done, and day after day everything remained untouched. I was despondent without Humphrey, for so long my constant shadow and eternal sun. I prayed for a wave of desire to wash over me and replace the incessant waves of dread.

The world went on around me—neighbors came and went, dogs visited the oak tree outside my living room window to do their business, kids played until dark in the park just beyond the creek—but inside I felt emotionally naked. Judging from my waistline though, I must have had enough energy to eat because most of my pants had become barely buttonable.

The slipcovers for the couch and the sofa chair had come back from the cleaners removed of Humphrey's hair, but I couldn't manage to take them out of the closet. Of all the furniture I owned, the couch had the strongest association with Humphrey. As the days went by, I thought it just as well to stick with the slipcoverless white couch. In my mind, the green chenille slipcovers would demand the return of Humphrey, salivating at my side for a bite of my Häagen-Dazs Vanilla Almond Fudge ice cream.

There were other things that I couldn't tend to as well: a heaping pile of boxes remained stacked in the hallway by the bathroom; a mountain of clothes, both dirty and clean, spilled off the sofa chair in the corner of my bedroom; my CDs sat in a box next to the armoire; and the surface of my coffee table was blanketed with bills, books, and miscellaneous papers. My framed photographs were scattered throughout the apartment, leaning against the walls. A particularly large one of Humphrey sitting on his favorite white bench in our backyard in Ojai was next to my bed, covered with a blanket. I avoided it like a scalding iron, unable to either store it away or hang it on the wall.

Odd behavior for someone who is normally distraught

by disorganization. But in some small way being unsettled made Humphrey's absence seem less permanent. I was creating another environment, like a friend's home or a motel room, that wasn't reminiscent of home, a place where Humphrey wasn't supposed to be. I could still irrationally reason with myself that this whole ordeal was just a long, sad vacation or a horrible dream. When it was over, I would be reunited with Humphrey. As much as this mindset kept me from healing, it helped me to move forward through another day.

Every morning when I fixed my tea, the tea kettle's whistle would instantly bring to mind Humphrey's face. For so long it had been a ritual that signaled the start of a new day—sitting with Humphrey on the couch, sipping a cup of green tea. Some days I welcomed the whistle as a warm reminder; on others I couldn't bear the sound and stood by the kettle, waiting to flip the lid open just before the whistle would blow.

Every time I returned to the apartment after having been away for a long stretch, I would forget that Humphrey was gone. Turning the key to the front door, I would expect him to be on the other side. When he wasn't, I would feel his presence, dancing with excitement in the entryway, straining to stick his nose into every grocery bag as he followed me toward the kitchen. I began a ritual of talking to him each time I came in, like I had always done.

To add to the reminders of Humphrey inside my apartment, a powerful one was about to make a home delivery. One morning on my way out to the grocery store, I opened the front door to find an oversized envelope at my feet. I walked back inside, gently opened the envelope, and removed its contents. I found myself holding an advanced copy of my first book.

I was filled with emotion as I turned the pages—Mollie, Max, Wally, Bailey, Bubba...all proudly representing senior dogs with dignity and grace. How strange to think that of all the projects I had pitched to publishers, the least commercial one had gotten published. Even stranger still was that among the many dogs that would pass on by the time the book was published, my own dog, just seven years old at the time, would be gone as well.

Although Humphrey was not the subject of the book, he was its spirit, and everything associated with the book brought him back to me. As I flipped through the last few pages I prepared myself for the author shot of Humphrey and me on the back flap. There it was—Humphrey, with a big smile, anxious to step out of the still photograph and play.

The natural world, as it had in Utah, would again pull me out of my shell. While it wasn't on the scale of Kanab's open and expansive beauty or the grandeur of a national park, a small rustic haven awaited me just beyond the crew-cut lawns, styled trees, and leaf-blown properties that defined suburbia.

Its entrance was hidden except for a metal crossbar just off the street curb that looked like a miniature football field goal post. The short trail, bordered on one side by fenced-in backyards and on the other by a creek, was rarely traveled, and in my daily morning and afternoon walks, I could go weeks seeing only a single dog being walked by its owner or a pair of joggers.

Bunny rabbits were usually my first sight after stepping off the concrete onto the brown earth. As skittish as they were adorable, the rabbits scampered for cover under nearby bushes with my slightest movement. I would always try to walk gently around them and talk softly in the hopes of gaining their trust and getting close, but I never succeeded. There weren't many open spaces in the area—on the trail and off—where you wouldn't see at least a couple of bunnies. Thinking back on my childhood, it's hard to believe how popular it was for kids to carry rabbits' feet, often as key chains, for good luck. I don't think any of us, at the time, made the association of where the cute little key chains emanated from.

Beyond the bunnies, across the creek, the trail began. A canopy of enormous oak trees spilled shade onto the winding, gently sloped dirt path, providing respite from the often hot valley sun. Birds and squirrels delighted in the dense green den, flitting about, using the trees as their home base for adventure. On occasion you could glimpse a gorgeous white egret standing in the center of the creek with its wings draped around itself like a wedding dress. I would stand for a while and watch it move its pencil-thin dainty legs through the water. (Imagine if we could walk through our crazy, hectic world with such grace, elegance, and beauty.)

What I loved most about the trail were the ducks. I don't know what it was exactly, certainly I'd seen ducks before, but I developed a particular bond with the Lindero Creek ducks. I loved to watch them paddle along as if skating on ice, with their adorable portly bodies, leaving a trail of tiny rippled waves behind, or see a group of them fly overhead quacking away.

After a couple of months of traveling the trail twice a day, I came across a pair of adult ducks with two ducklings sunning themselves on the side of the creek. I took a moment to congratulate the parents on the offspring and introduce myself to the little ones. When I crossed the creek to continue my walk, there was an animal-control person spraying the weeds off to the right of the path. I motioned a hello and the man looked at me strangely. He probably had been there the whole time, listening to me talk with my feathered friends. As I passed him, I was tempted to turn back and say, "Hey buddy, when's the last time you conversed with a creature that can walk, swim, and fly?"

My fascination with the ducks continued. Coming back to my apartment late one afternoon from a walk, I saw movement out of the corner of my eye toward the direction of the apartment complex pool. Having never seen even one person inside the gated area, much less take a swim, I first thought a couple of kids must be swimming. Looking over I was surprised to see a pair of ducks moving from the deep end to the shallow end like two floats in a parade.

I quickly learned that the ducks had a thing for our pool. Many mornings you could find them sleeping with their heads tucked against their bodies in the still water. There was one male duck that was fond of standing like a statue at dusk on the concrete edge of the pool near the diving board. He stood in the same exact spot every time, with unbroken concentration—a true Zen master. The duck was so still the first time I saw it that I had to get a closer look to be sure it was alive.

At the creek trail's end my walking route continued along a couple of residential streets before intersecting with an open field behind a large, modern church. Unlike the creek trail, this was an open dirt path bordered on both sides by backyards, with no trees, no water, and no ducks. It seemed strange to see such wonderous backyards with sprawling lawns, swing-sets, and swimming pools, yet rarely see any kids outside playing. I suppose in today's world kids are more apt to be in front of a computer game or the TV set.

There was one backyard in particular that I always approached with great anticipation. Without fail, at the sound of my footsteps or my voice singing along with my Walkman, my canine welcoming committee would come running—one yellow Lab and one black Lab, identical in age and size—toward the wrought iron gate. The two of them would then run back and forth along the gate in a rousing welcome, their tails wagging like flags in the wind.

Boy, what a joyous sight it is to see dogs. Wherever I come across them—sitting upright in the passenger seat of a car, plopped down on a storefront welcome mat, or milling about in a neighbor's yard—they always bring a smile to my face.

Shortly after moving into my new neighborhood, I wandered over to the local animal shelter.

As far as shelters go, it was a pleasing one. It was cradled between civilization and nature, with a bustling freeway on one side and a serene mountain range on the other. Built in the fifties, the rectangular building that housed the dogs contained a single row of forty small concrete cages, about three-quarters of them filled with what looked like sweet, lovable pooches. Encircling the building were five fenced grass runs of generous size filled with chew toys and tennis balls. Each run had a vinyl canopy tent with a couple of plastic lawn chairs to provide a break from the brutal summer heat of the valley. One of the volunteers, tending to a five-month-old German shepherd with big goofy ears, informed me that the shelter has the fourth highest adoption rate among shelters in the United States.

After a quick walk-through and a pep talk to each dog—"What a gorgeous girl! Keep your spirits up, you'll find a good home soon"—I started back for my car. As I opened the gate leading out of the shelter area, I passed by a volunteer holding two puppies followed by a woman with a small child. The volunteer turned to me and said, "I don't know what type of dog you're looking for, but they just brought these puppies from Pasadena and they're awesome dogs—real sweet." The mother and child followed the volunteer through the side entrance of the administration building.

I decided to wait outside until they reappeared. While the woman filled out adoption paperwork for one of the puppies, the volunteer, Robin, came back with the remaining available pup. Judging by its coloring—black and brown with white below her nose, on her chest, and on the tips of her paws—Robin guessed the female pup might have some Australian shepherd in her.

Robin handed me the puppy to hold. She was incredibly docile, looking like a three-year-old child in need of a nap, perhaps pooped from her long transport from Pasadena. As I stroked the puppy's soft fur, Robin gauged my interest in the dog. I filled her in about Humphrey and shared with her my experience at Best Friends.

Robin intimately understood my hardship—she had previously owned two dogs that had both died from bloat. In both cases, which occurred at separate times, the dogs were in her care at the time they became ill. Picking up on the signals of discomfort the dogs displayed, she was able, in each scenario, to immediately rush them to her nearby vet. Both dogs successfully underwent the excruciating surgery, which has a fifty-fifty success rate, and the vet assured her in each case that they had made it through the horrible ordeal. Sadly, their fates were parallel—both dogs died days later while in post operative care at the vet's office. The second case had so devastated the vet that he had called Robin in tears to tell her the awful news.

Robin implored me not to feel guilty about Humphrey's death. "Mark, I was able to get my dogs immediate medical attention and I still lost them both," she said. The ailment that had inflicted her dogs, and Humphrey, sounded akin to a human having a brain aneurysm or some other affliction that they are genetically predisposed to. It made me realize for the first time that even had I been with Humphrey while he suffered from bloat, there is no guarantee I could have saved his life.

After we finished sharing our emotional stories, Robin agreed to place a hold on the pup until 10 A.M. the next morning so I could have some time to think on it.

Back at my apartment I began the self-torture that accompanies any major decision in my life—an agonizing marathon of arguing for and against something like a razor-sharp attorney with a split personality.

Some people are too close to their lives; others too far away. I'm definitely too close, overexamining my every move, fearful of making a mistake, painting a dozen possible outcomes before any have a chance to unfold. Intellectually I have long understood that life is an uncrackable mystery, not an exact science, and although I've worked hard on quieting my mind, it can still put up a pretty good fight.

The next morning, on my way back to the shelter, I was nervous and excited, mulling over the possibility of beginning anew with another dog. With the mad attorney still arguing the case in my head, I found the two pups from yesterday in a small run in the kennel area. I unlatched the gate and as fast as I scooted in, the pups rushed me—jumping on my pant legs, biting at my shoe- laces, and vying against each other for my attention. Boy, were these pups a far cry from the sleepyheads they had been the day before! Five minutes and a severed shoelace later, the woman whom I had met yesterday came over to pick up her pup, now spayed and ready to go home.

Now it was just me and the unclaimed pup. I picked her up, cradled her against my chest, and kissed her head. I tried to let the moment just *be*, but the moment quickly filled up with questions: Was I ready? Was this *the* one? How smart would this dog turn out to be? How would she look full-grown? Was she healthy?

Putting the puppy down and watching her amble around, I thought about Humphrey's inauspicious beginnings. I never could have imagined he would turn out to be such a rare, intelligent, and responsive dog.

I wandered over to the kennel area to get out of my head for a few minutes.

There was a part of me that wanted to take home every dog I saw—from Leo, the fourteen-year-old German shepherd, a stoic, gentle giant with the wisest eyes I've ever seen, to Buster, a beautiful black chow mix with every attribute but a loving owner. But there was a greater part of me that was scared to care for one dog again the way I had cared for Humphrey.

I had been told by countless dog people that I would know when I found the right dog. But I was starting to realize, in my association with dogs at Best Friends and afterward, that I was trying to replace Humphrey, not find a new dog. Certainly a natural reaction considering my circumstances, but it made the criteria for selecting a new dog near impossible. No dog, no matter how cute, inquisitive, or intelligent was going to be able to instantly take Humphrey's place. Our bond had been rich in years and experiences. To compare a new dog with Humphrey would be unfair, to the dog and to me.

Perhaps, for now, volunteering would be best, I thought. It would give me the opportunity to spread my love to many dogs without investing emotionally in just one. If I were to take a dog home, I knew I would dedicate myself wholeheartedly to training, loving, and assimilating that dog into my life; most likely there would be little time left for volunteering.

I felt sad leaving the sweet pup behind, but I was looking forward to doing my small part to make the lives of the many dogs in those tiny, cold cages a little warmer. I walked back into the administration building, told the staff of my decision to pass on the pup, and signed up for a regular volunteer shift.

I believe you can measure the heart of a city by the way it treats its animals. My new town scored high. I was amazed by the volume of people who passed through the shelter during my weekday volunteer hours, inquiring about the welfare of the dogs, adopting dogs of all sizes and ages, and bringing their own dogs to the shelter to be sure the dogs approved of their owners' potential adoptions.

The shelter's volunteer staff was equally dedicated to the dogs. In addition to the regular county employees, there were at least two volunteers at the shelter throughout the day to socialize with the dogs and let them out of their cages to play in the fenced-in runs. Several volunteers even took dogs with medical needs to their own private vets, to illicit attention beyond what they felt the shelter vets were providing. I'd venture to guess that the dogs at the shelter were doted on more than many seniors in retirement homes.

Over the next few months of volunteering, I witnessed many touching incidents at the shelter, but one sticks out.

One hot Monday afternoon, Susan, a fellow volunteer, led me to a cage toward the back of the building. There I laid eyes on Rudy, a twelve-year-old mutt who was part golden retriever and all love. He was overweight (Susan indicated he may have liver problems), incredibly stiff, and shaking. I helped Susan lift Rudy over the metal frame below the door in order to get him out of his cage. I then led him to one of the larger fenced runs. I stayed with him for a long while, giving him gentle rubs behind his ears and throwing him a tennis ball, which he slowly chased and returned. To give him a break from his tiny, hot cage, Susan and I decided to let him stay in the run for the rest of the afternoon.

Throughout the remaining hours the shelter was open,

several people noticed Rudy in the run and stepped inside to say hello. By day's end, a young couple walked over to me while I was tending to another dog in an adjoining run and said they were interested in sharing their home with Rudy. The satisfaction I felt leading Rudy out to the couple's car is beyond the realm of words; the renewed faith I felt in the compassion of people had me teary-eyed as I walked from the parking lot back through the shelter entrance.

Despite touching success stories like Rudy's and the high adoption rate the shelter enjoyed, there were still a few candidates that could use some help. Shep, a German shepherd mix somewhere between three and five years old, was in need. He had been at the shelter the longest of any of the dogs, five months, and had had an extensive stay at another shelter before being transferred over. He was extremely sweet but increasingly depressed by his extended shelter stays—his ribs were beginning to show through his beige and black coat.

Every time visitors walked through the shelter and the place erupted with barking, poor Shep would sit silently with his hind legs shaking. If his appearance and demeanor didn't turn off potential adopters, his routine of peeing on the green lawn chair in the run, where interested parties sat, may have.

Knowing Shep's time at the shelter couldn't go on forever—he needed to be adopted or else he might be put down—I decided to call Debbie, a woman I had met at Best Friends. She had had the arduous task of deciding which dogs to take in among the 2,000 placement requests the organization received annually from rescue groups, shelters, and individuals.

In my opening pitch for Shep I said, "I know you get countless calls to help, but this dog is different." I thought my approach was working fairly well—I had established a sympathetic understanding of her dilemma—but Debbie quickly spotted me as a newcomer to the cause and said, "Mark, do you realize how many dogs you're going to come across that you want to save?" I kept to my mission—Save Shep—and after some more of my rambling, Debbie told me to find out a couple more bits of information about the dog and get back to her. She promised she would keep an open mind.

The news was soon to get much better for Shep. Before Robin, the now dog-anointed head volunteer, was able to take him through the paces of a temperament test and see how he fared in close proximity with other dogs, a grandfather came into the shelter with his ten-year-old grandson and adopted him. On cue, Shep promptly peed on the chair where the grandfather was sitting. It didn't matter—Shep was going home!

The months flew by for me—dog days to be sure— filled with photo shoots, new book projects involving dogs, and volunteering at the animal shelter. Even on my writing days, committed to completing this story, I was serenaded every afternoon by Summit—a three-year-old cheery yellow Lab that lived below me—with a bellowing baritone howl. I still didn't have a new dog, but an incident occurred that signaled to me I was close to taking the plunge.

It happened just after I had arrived at the shelter to begin another volunteer shift. Walking the row of cages, as I always did first thing, I found myself staring at two jet-black Labs with warm hazel-colored eyes, adorably collapsed against one another in a fitful sleep. They awoke and pushed off each other and sauntered my way, with their short stocky bodies, to lick me hello through their cage.

The on-staff vet, who would be the enemy of any aspiring starlet because of his age estimates, pegged the Labs to be around three years old. They struck Susan, the other volunteer on-staff, and me as being no more than a year old. Incredibly, they had come in as strays.

Sensing I was smitten with the dogs, Susan quickly pointed to the two red house stickers placed on their paperwork, which was clipped to the cage. The houses signified a hold on a dog if no one claimed it within five business days. Susan added that there were at least seven other people interested in the dogs. People can be flaky, I thought, but passing on these dogs would be like a kid turning down a golden ticket to Wonkaland.

When I volunteered again a week later, I was stunned to hear that everyone had dropped off the wait list and that the Labs were claimed by two separate parties—a family with two young children and a young couple—just before I had arrived.

Talking with Robin later on the phone that night, I learned that the shelter, by law, could only record two names, and if those people didn't come to adopt the dogs on the date they became available, the dogs were available to anyone.

The Labs had alerted me that I was ready, at last, for another dog. They had broken through the endless chatter of my mind and reached my bruised and hardened heart.

Not long after the incident, I discovered Petfinders.com and entered the World Wide Web of canine adoption possibilities. In no time I was dizzy with dogs—shooting off emails to inquire about a certain dog's availability, marking my calendar to attend rescue group adoption events, and talking to fellow dog lovers over the phone. It wouldn't be long now.

As July approached I got an email from Robin letting the volunteers know that a group was forming to visit a neighboring animal shelter to comfort its dogs on the Fourth of July. The shelter's location was 150 feet from the Lion's Club, ground zero for the launch of a lively and loud fireworks display. The previous year the dogs were extremely distraught by the deafening noise and a couple

had injured themselves trying to escape their environment.

On America's birthday, I caravanned with a small
group of dog lovers to the shelter, a half-hour's drive
north. We arrived with enough remaining daylight to take
each dog out for a stroll and a short recess in one of the
grass runs. Before long the dark canvas of sky was filled
with exploding light and sound. With Gypsy, a five-year-
old German shorthair, sitting next to me on the lawn
inside the run, slightly bemused by the sky show, I drifted
off in thought.

It had been seven months now since Humphrey's
death, and with the passage of time the sharp pain and
deep void I experienced as a result of his passing had
lessened. The endless cycle of questions regarding how
and why Humphrey had to die had become less prevalent.
I no longer felt guilty about my role in his death but
instead focused on the role I had played in his life and the
role he had played in mine.

With Gypsy by my side, licking my hand, the final
spurt of fireworks splintered across the sky and faded
away.

# NOTE TO READER

Thank you for reading *Humphrey Was Here*. It was difficult to put down my experience in words, but I'm so glad I did. I've received countless emails from dog lovers who, during a difficult time, were comforted by the book. Many people have asked me if I got another dog after Humphrey passed away. It took me a little over a year, but the time was right, and the wait was worth it, when I adopted Payton. If you get a chance, come meet him on my website.

www.markjasher.com/payton

Made in the USA
Lexington, KY
21 August 2013